the greatest
Soccer Players
of all time

the greatest Soccer Players of all time

TOM MACDONALD

INTRODUCTION BY GAVIN HAMILTON

southwater

This edition is published by Southwater

Southwater is an imprint of Anness Publishing Limited, Hermes House,
88–89 Blackfriars Road, London SE1 8HA, tel. 020 7401 2077; fax 020 7633 9499;
www.southwaterbooks.com; info@anness.com

© Anness Publishing Ltd 2003

UK agent: The Manning Partnership Ltd, 6 The Old Dairy, Melcombe Road, Bath BA2 3LR;
tel. 01225 478444; fax 01225 478440; sales@manning-partnership.co.uk

UK distributor: Grantham Book Services Ltd, Isaac Newton Way, Alma Park Industrial Estate,
Grantham, Lincs NG31 9SD; tel. 01476 541080; fax 01476 541061; orders@gbs.tbs-ltd.co.uk

North American agent/distributor: National Book Network, 4501 Forbes Boulevard, Suite 200,
Lanham, MD 20706; tel. 301 459 3366; fax 301 429 5746; www.nbnbooks.com

Australian agent/distributor: Pan Macmillan Australia, Level 18, St Martins Tower, 31 Market St,
Sydney, NSW 2000; tel. 1300 135 113; fax 1300 135 103; customer.service@macmillan.com.au

New Zealand agent/distributor: David Bateman Ltd, 30 Tarndale Grove, Off Bush Road, Albany,
Auckland; tel. (09) 415 7664; fax (09) 415 8892

A CIP catalogue record for this book is available from the British Library.

Publisher Joanna Lorenz
Managing Editor Judith Simons
Senior Editor Sarah Ainley
Text Editors Richard Rosenfeld and Peter Arnold
Designers Paul Wright and Nigel Partridge
Jacket Design Balley Design
Production Controller Darren Price

PICTURE CREDITS
All images supplied by **Colorsport** except for the following:
t = top; b = bottom; c = center; l = left; r = right
Empics All jacket images, 1, 2, 3, 4l, 4c, 4r, 5t, 5b, 6t, 6b, 7tl, 7tr, 7bl, 27, 29t, 36b, 38t, 39t, 48t, 48b,
51b, 62, 70b, 72b, 73t, 89b.
Hulton Getty 10b, 26b, 40t, 59t, 71b, 74b, 84b.
Popperfoto 22b, 24t, 30b, 34b, 47c, 50t, 55b, 76b, 81b, 84b, 88.

10 9 8 7 6 5 4 3 2 1

*Page 1: Argentina's Diego Maradona
at the Mexico World Cup in 1986.*

*Page 2: Brazil and Real Madrid striker,
Ronaldo, voted World Footballer of the
Year in 2003.*

*Page 3: Brazil's Pele watches as France
goalkeeper Claude Abbes pounces on
the ball in the World Cup Semi-final of
1958 in Sweden.*

*Page 4: (left) Liverpool's Michael Owen;
(centre) Tottenham Hotspur's Jürgen
Klinsmann; (right) Manchester United's
Ryan Giggs.*

*Page 5: (top right) Real Madrid's new
signing, David Beckham; (below left)
West Ham United captain Bobby Moore
holds aloft the FA Cup trophy after his
team's 3–2 victory over Preston North
End in 1964.*

Contents

Introduction

The players are football's most valuable assets. Without them, there would be no game. They are the game's ultimate stars and they deserve to be recognized.

Through the decades, there have been many great players who have lit up the game with their brilliance. But how do you define true greatness? What sets apart truly great players from the very good ones? Success at the World Cup is as good a measure as any.

Pelé, the greatest of them all, won three World Cups, in 1958, 1962 and 1970. That feat could yet be emulated by Ronaldo, already twice a winner, in 1994 and 2002, and he's still only 26 years old. Argentina's Diego Maradona, in 1986, and Zinedine Zidane of France, in 1998, were the inspiration behind their country's World Cup victories.

It is not just forwards who have savoured World Cup glory. Lest we forget the contribution of Bobby Moore, in England in 1966, Franz Beckenbauer in West Germany in 1974 and Lothar Matthäus with Germany in 1990.

Of course, some of the game's greatest players have never won the World Cup. Johan Cruyff, majestic and mercurial for Holland, was a losing finalist in 1974.

Above: West Germany's captain Franz Beckenbauer (left) in 1974.

Below: Pele's shot is saved by the Italian keeper in the 1970 World Cup Final.

Above: Ronaldo (left) was instrumental in Brazil's 2002 World Cup triumph.

Above: Real Madrid line up before a pre-season friendly in China in 2003.

Michel Platini, the wonderful artist, tasted success with France in the 1984 European Championship but never on the world stage.

Others never even played in the World Cup finals. George Best, representing Northern Ireland, did not come close. Alfredo Di

Below: The 2003 AC Milan side have plenty to celebrate: winning major competitions such as the Champions League adds to a player's value.

Stefano, who played for both Spain and Argentina, and George Weah, arguably the greatest African footballer of all time, were both far more influential at club level.

Di Stefano is considered by many who saw him in full flow to be the greatest ever player of all time. His biggest achievements came in the early years of the European Cup, in the 1950s, when Real Madrid won five trophies in a row.

Di Stefano was not the only star in that Real Madrid team. Players of the calibre of Ferenc Puskas, Didi and Gento also graced the most successful club side in football history. Almost half a century later, Real Madrid are trying to emulate the achievements of the 1950s by gathering together the greatest collection of superstar players ever to have been featured in one side at the same time.

The 2003 vintage of Real Madrid contains a positive galaxy of world class performers, including the last three World Footballers of the Year, Ronaldo, Zidane and Luis Figo, as well as the most photographed player on the planet, England's David Beckham, and two of the most successful, Spain's Raul and the Brazilian, Roberto Carlos.

As the popularity of football continues to grow, so the status of the star players is enhanced. They are now richer and better rewarded than ever before. But the corresponding pressures are more intense, and they surely work hard for the accolades and the glory that are heaped upon them.

A–Z GREAT PLAYERS

This book looks at the club and international careers of the world's greatest players, past and present. From Florian Albert to Andoni Zubizarreta, the roll call is a glittering one and, although one can argue about the criteria for inclusion (argument and disagreement are at the heart of football discussions), there is little doubt that these players deserve a place in the top echelon of footballing history. Transfer dates, number of caps and international goals have been given where possible.

Florian Albert
(Hungary, b. 1941)

Clubs: *Ferencvaros (1956–74)*
Caps: *75 (27 goals)*

A naturally gifted, multi-talented centre-forward, Albert's ability was noticed by the youth coaches at Ferencvaros soon after his family's move to Budapest from the country, while Albert was still a young boy. He made his debut for Ferencvaros at the age of 16 and gained his first cap for Hungary, in 1958, in a 3–2 defeat of Sweden. His pace, dribbling ability and scoring prowess, with either foot,

Left: The naturally talented goal scorer, Florian Albert, in action for Hungary in the 1960s.

quickly established him as a Hungarian footballing hero with club and country. In his long career with Ferencvaros he won four league winner's medals, and he was three times Hungary's top goal scorer. He played in the 1962 World Cup finals, where he scored against England, and he claimed a hat trick in Hungary's 6–1 rout of Bulgaria, although Hungary were eliminated in the quarter-finals. In the 1966 World Cup finals, Albert produced an electrifying individual display when Hungary beat Brazil 3–1, though again they could not get beyond the quarter-finals. He retired from international football in 1971, having been voted European Footballer of the Year in 1967, in honour of his outstanding performance in the World Cup finals the previous year.

José Altafini
(Brazil, b. 1938)

Clubs: *Palmeiras (1956–58), AC Milan (1958–65), Napoli (1965–72), Juventus (1972–76), Chiasso (1976)*
Caps: *8 (4 goals) Brazil; 6 (5) Italy*

Altafini was a strong, opportunistic centre-forward, who first made his mark as a 19 year old in the 1958 World Cup finals. Known in Brazil as "Mazzola" for his resemblance to Valentino, the captain of Torino killed in the 1949 Superga air crash, he was bought by AC Milan. He then readopted his birth name and played for Italy in the 1962 World Cup finals, becoming one of only four players to have represented two countries in the tournament. He was a prolific scorer for AC Milan and was the top scorer in the 1963 European Cup with 14 goals, scoring two in the final against Benfica at Wembley. He moved on to Napoli shortly after, and then to Juventus, for whom he played at the age of 35 in the 1973 European Cup Final, which the Italian club lost 1–0 to Ajax. Altafini finished his career with Swiss league club Chiasso.

Above: Two-time European Cup finalist José Altafini playing for his adopted country, Italy, where he played most of his club football.

Osvaldo Ardiles
(Argentina, b. 1952)

Clubs: *Instituto de Cordoba (1969–74), Huracan (1974–78), Tottenham Hotspur (1978–82), Paris Saint-Germain (1982–83), Tottenham Hotspur (1983–88), Blackburn Rovers (1988), Queens Park Rangers (1988–89)*
Caps: *53 (8 goals)*

Ardiles, Argentina's star midfield player in the country's successful 1978 World Cup, stunned British football when, with fellow Argentinian Ricky Villa, he joined Spurs in the summer of that year. His sparkling ability, unselfish play and modest self-deprecation made "Ossie" a great crowd favourite at White Hart Lane, and he helped Spurs

Above: Ossie Ardiles, playing for his country in the 1978 World Cup Finals.

lift the 1981 FA Cup in a 3–2 replay win over Manchester City. He missed the final the following year due to the Falklands War, and went on loan to Paris Saint-Germain before rejoining Spurs in early 1983, having played in the 1982 World Cup finals. He played in Spurs' victorious 1984 UEFA Cup campaign when they beat Anderlecht on penalties, and left the club in 1988 to join Queens Park Rangers. He became manager of Swindon in 1989 and then took over at Newcastle United in 1991, but he was sacked the following year. He became manager at West Bromwich Albion and left the "Baggies" in June 1993 to rejoin Spurs. However, his defensive shortcomings brought him the sack again 16 months later. He then coached Croatia Zagreb and Yokohama F. Marinos (Japan) until 2001.

Roberto Baggio
(Italy, b. 1967)

Clubs: *Vicenza (1982–85), Fiorentina (1985–90), Juventus (1990–95), AC Milan (1995–97), Bologna (1997–98), Inter Milan (1998–2000), Brescia (2000–)*
Caps: *55 (27 goals)*

Baggio, the "Divine Ponytail", is a forward of the highest class and was, at one time, the finest player in the world. Slight, skilful and a natural scorer, he became a star with Fiorentina and set a new world transfer record with his £8 million move to Juventus in 1990. His goals helped the Turin club to the *Serie A* title in 1995 and the UEFA Cup in 1993, the year he was voted World and European Footballer of the Year. He had a brilliant World Cup in 1990 and, with Brazil's Romario, was player of the tournament in the 1994 World Cup. His miss in the penalty shoot-out in the final gave the Brazilians the trophy. The arrival of Alessandro Del Piero hastened Baggio's departure to AC Milan in 1995, and his transfer to Bologna in 1997 was followed by a move to Inter Milan in 1998, and then to Brescia in 2000.

Above: Italian forward Roberto Baggio, "little prince" of the Azzurri and World Footballer of the Year in 1993.

Gordon Banks
(England, b. 1937)

Clubs: *Chesterfield (1955–59), Leicester City (1959–67), Stoke City (1967–75), Fort Lauderdale Strikers (1977–78)*
Caps: *73*

England's greatest-ever goalkeeper, Gordon Banks was a tall, dependable, agile stopper. He joined Leicester in 1959 and played on the losing side in the 1961 and 1963 FA Cup Finals, winning the League Cup in 1964, an achievement he repeated with Stoke City in 1972. He was in goal for England in their 1966 triumph in the World Cup Final, having made his international debut in 1963. Banks represented his country again in the 1970 World Cup in Mexico and is best remembered for his marvellous save from a disbelieving Pelé against Brazil, still called "the save of the century". He was awarded an OBE in 1970. Affectionately known as "Banks of England", he was voted Footballer of the Year in 1973. A car crash that year meant he lost the sight in his right eye, although he played one more season with Fort Lauderdale before retiring.

Above: George Best closes in on England's Gordon Banks.

Franceschino Baresi
(Italy, b. 1960)

Club: *AC Milan (1977–97)*
Caps: *81 (1 goal)*

Franco Baresi, the great sweeper and magisterial organizer of Arrigo Sacchi's marvellous AC Milan side, together with Costacurta and Paolo Maldini, provided the defensive platform for the scoring talents of, among others, Marco Van Basten, Ruud Gullit and Dejan Savicevic. A perceptive and intelligent centre-back, Baresi made his league debut in 1978 and remained with the club in its fallow period, until Silvio Berlusconi's millions made it one of the top clubs in Europe. He won six league titles and two European Cups with Milan, in 1989 and 1990, but was suspended for the 1994 final with Barcelona. He received his first cap in 1982 but, in his international career, he was overshadowed by the presence of Juventus' Gaetano Scirea as sweeper until the last years of that decade. He played in the 1990 World Cup finals hosted by Italy and, four years later, came close to lifting the World Cup trophy for his country as captain. Baresi's performance at USA '94 was all the more memorable (in spite of missing his first penalty in the shoot-out against Brazil in the final) because he had undergone surgery on his knee just two weeks before the tournament began. Franco Baresi retired in 1997.

Right: Franco Baresi, the rock of the defence for AC Milan and Italy.

Above: Cliff "Boy" Bastin in the famous old Arsenal strip.

Cliff Bastin
(England, 1912–91)

Clubs: Exeter City (1927–29), Arsenal (1929–46)
Caps: 21 (12 goals)

Left-winger Cliff Bastin was only 16 years old when Arsenal manager Herbert Chapman spotted him playing for Third Division Exeter City. By the time he was 20, "Boy" Bastin, as he was nicknamed, had won every honour in the English game with Arsenal. He was the youngest player to play in a Cup Final in Arsenal's 1930 defeat of Huddersfield Town, and in his time with the London club he won another Cup medal in 1936 and five league medals. Playing up front with forwards Jack Lambert and David Jack, and supplied from midfield by the impishly skilful Alex James, Bastin's ball skills, pace and directness brought him a hatful of goals, including 28 in the 1930–31 season, and 33 in 1932–33. He held the record for the number of goals scored for Arsenal (178) until overtaken by Ian Wright in 1997–98. Cliff Bastin died in 1991.

Gabriel Batistuta
(Argentina, b. 1969)

Clubs: Newells Old Boys (1988–89), River Plate (1989–90), Boca Juniors (1990–91), Fiorentina (1991–2000), Roma (2000–)
Caps: 78 (56 goals)

The long-haired centre-forward Batistuta was a revered figure in his adopted city of Florence. With a statue in his honour at the club's Stadio Communale, Fiorentina was proud of "Batigol's" tremendous goal-scoring feats and his loyalty to the club. Before joining Fiorentina, Batistuta played his football in Argentina, and his six goals in the *Copa America* helped his country win the South American tournament. At Fiorentina, he quickly became the leading scorer, scoring 13 goals in his first season. He is also Argentina's highest-ever goal scorer with a tally of 56. Batistuta played for his country in the 1994, 1998 and 2002 World Cup finals but retired from the international game in 2002. He left Fiorentina for Roma in 2000, but was transferred on loan to Inter Milan in 2003.

Above: Gabriel Batistuta on the attack.

Left: Scotland's "Slim Jim" Baxter.

Jim Baxter
(Scotland, 1939–2001)

Clubs: Raith Rovers (1957–60), Rangers (1960–65), Sunderland (1965–67), Nottingham Forest (1967–69), Rangers (1969–70)
Caps: 34 (3 goals)

"Slim Jim" Baxter was probably the most skilful left-sided footballer ever to have come out of Scotland. His immaculate passing, vision and ability to ghost through defences at will, marked him out as a player of genius. An idol to the Rangers fans of the 1960s, he was the playmaker in the all-conquering team that won three league championships, three Scottish Cups and four Scottish League Cups between 1960 and 1965, including the "treble" in 1964. Baxter left Rangers in 1965, just as Celtic were starting to challenge Rangers' dominance in the Scottish league. He moved across the border to England, but his brilliance only showed itself fitfully. Baxter never had the chance to demonstrate his class in the World Cup finals. However, Scottish football fans still remember his two goals past England's debutant keeper Gordon Banks in 1963 at Wembley, and his masterful performance against the "auld enemy" in 1967 when, along with Denis Law, he inspired a 3–2 win over England, the then World Champions. In 1969, Baxter returned to Rangers, and he made his retirement from football the following year. He died in 2001.

Franz Beckenbauer
(Germany, b. 1945)

Clubs: *Bayern Munich (1964–77), New York Cosmos (1977–80), Hamburg (1980–82), New York Cosmos (1983)*
Caps: *103 (14 goals)*

"*Der Kaiser*", the attacking sweeper for Bayern Munich and West Germany, had a profound influence on German football in the 1960s and 1970s. An elegant player with slide-rule distribution, Beckenbauer made his debut for Bayern in 1964 and played on the losing side in the 1966 World Cup Final at Wembley. However, he scored in West Germany's 3–2 quarter-final victory over England in the 1970 tournament and, supported by the skills of Günter Netzer, he led his country to their European Championship triumph in 1972, when he was named European Footballer of the Year. He captained his country to further success in the 1974 World Cup Final, beating Johann Cruyff's great Dutch team 2–1, and he inspired Bayern to three European Cups in succession from 1974–76. In 1976 he was voted European Footballer of the Year for the second time, and the following year he moved to the United States to join New York Cosmos. He became West Germany's manager in 1984 and led the side to their 1986 World Cup Final defeat by Argentina. He managed the team to victory in the 1990 World Cup Final, though, becoming the first man both to captain and manage a World Cup-winning team. Beckenbauer is currently club president at Bayern.

Right: Franz Beckenbauer initiates another attack for West Germany.

David Beckham
(England, b. 1975)

Clubs: *Manchester United (1993–2003), Real Madrid (2003–)*
Caps: *59 (10 goals)*

London-born Beckham played his first league game for Manchester United in 1995 and quickly became a regular midfield provider to Alex Ferguson's attack. He is particularly adept at pinpoint crosses, and his ability to convert free kicks is unsurpassed in British football. He gained his first cap in 1996, and achieved both fame and notoriety in the 1998 World Cup finals: after a fine free kick against Colombia, he got sent off against Argentina for a petulant kick on Diego Simeone. Something of a media star after his marriage to pop singer "Posh Spice", Beckham gave composed performances in the European Cup for Manchester United, and his injury-time goal from a free-kick against Greece in the last qualifier for the 2002 World Cup won England a place in the finals. Beckham has five League, two FA Cup and one European Cup winner's medals to his name. Amid a media frenzy, United sold him to Real Madrid in 2003.

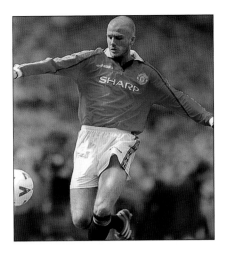

Above: David Beckham about to curl in one of his trademark crosses.

Above: Dennis Bergkamp, one of Holland's finest attackers in the 1990s.

Dennis Bergkamp
(Holland, b. 1969)

Clubs: *Ajax (1981–93), Inter Milan (1993–95), Arsenal (1995–)*
Caps: *79 (36 goals)*

Bergkamp is a forward with guile, speed and a delicate touch, who is both an unselfish creator and a predatory finisher. Named after Denis Law, he made his Ajax debut under manager Cruyff at the age of 17. By the time he left Ajax to join Inter Milan in 1993, he had scored 103 league goals for the Amsterdam side and won a UEFA Cup medal in Ajax's 1992 defeat of Torino. His talents were utilized only rarely by the Italian club, and three years later he was brought to Arsenal for £7.5 million. He took a few games to settle in at Highbury but, forging a striking partnership with Ian Wright, he soon became a cult figure with the London club. In 1997–98 his 22 goals helped Arsenal to secure the "double", and he was named Footballer of the Year that season. He was also vital in Arsenal's "double" of 2001–02. He gained his first cap in 1990, and despite his much-publicized fear of flying, played for Holland until Euro 2000. His sensational, last-minute winning goal in the 1998 World Cup quarter-finals against Argentina will live long in football fans' memories.

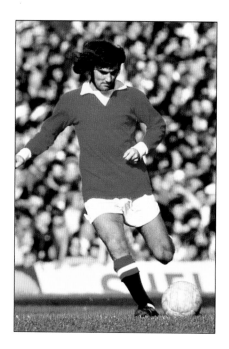

Above: The multi-talented George Best in action for Manchester United.

George Best
(N. Ireland, b. 1946)

Clubs: *Manchester United (1963–74), Fulham (1976–78), Fort Lauderdale Strikers (1978–79), Hibernian (1979–81), Bournemouth (1982)*
Caps: *37 (9 goals)*

Best was a supremely gifted player whose talents were eventually squandered by his off-pitch problems. A fast, skilful forward, he could also tackle and defend when necessary, and he scored some audacious and important goals for Manchester United. He made his debut for the club at the age of 17 and soon became the first "pop star" footballer, his "swinging sixties" lifestyle regularly attracting the attention of the tabloid press. He scored twice in United's 5–1 thrashing of Benfica in the 1966 European Cup quarter-final, and he scored United's second with a marvellous extra-time goal when they again defeated Benfica in the 1968 European Cup Final. That year, he was European Footballer of the Year and was top English league scorer with 28 goals. United's influence over English football began to wane and Best left the club in 1974, having played over 350 games for United and won two English league winner's medals. He gained 37 caps for Northern Ireland but never played at the highest international level. He came back into the game briefly with Fulham in 1976, and then played for a number of British and American clubs before retiring in 1982.

Danny Blanchflower
(N. Ireland, 1926–93)

Clubs: *Glentoran (1945–49), Barnsley (1949–51), Aston Villa (1951–54), Tottenham Hotspur (1954–64)*
Caps: *56 (2 goals)*

Captain of Spurs and Northern Ireland, right-half Blanchflower radiated style and authority. He was at the heart of the successful Spurs side of the early 1960s, and his subtle but effective distribution, and ability to control the game, inspired Spurs to their greatest triumph. Under his visionary leadership, Spurs became the first side in the 20th century to achieve the "double" of League and FA Cup in 1961, and they won the Cup again the following year. In 1963 they were the first British team to win a European trophy when they beat Atlético Madrid 5–1 to win the Cup Winners Cup. Blanchflower made his international debut in 1949, and the highlight of his Northern Ireland career was captaining his country to the quarter-finals of the 1958 World Cup. He retired in 1964 to become a journalist; his foray into management was less productive.

Above: Spurs' captain and inspiration Danny Blanchflower clears an attack.

Oleg Blokhin
(Soviet Union, b. 1952)

Clubs: *Kiev Dynamo,*
Vorwärts Steyr
Caps: *101 (39 goals)*

Blokhin was the former Soviet Union's most-capped player, and also the country's highest scorer. He began his career with Kiev Dynamo as a speedy left-winger (it is said he chose football over an athletics career as a sprinter), and gradually moved into the centre-forward position, where his pace and eye for goal helped Dynamo to seven Soviet league victories between 1974 and 1986. He scored in two Cup Winners' Cup Finals for Dynamo, beating Ferencvaros 3–0 in 1975, and beating Atlético Madrid by the

same score in 1986. After being granted permission to move to Western Europe, he played out the last years of his career with the Austrian club Vorwärts Steyr. Blokhin made his international debut in 1972, and played in both the 1982 and 1986 World Cup finals. He was the first Soviet player to play more than 100 games for his country, scoring 39 goals in his 101 international appearances. Blokhin was voted European Footballer of the Year in 1975. After his playing career had ended, Blokhin became manager of the Greek club side Olympiakos.

Right: Striker Oleg Blokhin, the Soviet Union's most-capped player.

Above: Zbigniew Boniek on the offensive for Juventus.

Zbigniew Boniek
(Poland, b. 1956)

Clubs: *Zawisa Bydgoszcz*
(1971–75), Widzew Lodz (1975–82),
Juventus (1982–85), Roma
(1985–88)
Caps: *80 (24 goals)*

Recognized as one of the finest Polish players ever, Boniek gained his first cap in 1976 and represented his country in the 1978 World Cup finals. He played again in 1982 and scored a hat trick in Poland's 3–0 defeat of Belgium in the second round, although he was injured for the semi-final elimination by the eventual winners, Italy. His prolific scoring abilities caught the attention of Juventus, who that year paid a then-record fee of £1.1 million to Widzew Lodz. Boniek played in the 1983 European Cup Final, when Juventus were beaten 1–0 by Hamburg, and he scored the winner in their 2–1 win over Portuguese side Porto in the 1984 Cup Winners' Cup Final. He also played in Juventus' 1–0 defeat of Liverpool in the 1985 European Cup Final. Boniek was voted European Footballer of the Year in 1982. He scored 24 goals in 80 international matches for Poland.

Liam Brady
(Ireland, b. 1956)

Clubs: *Arsenal (1973–80), Juventus (1980–82), Sampdoria (1982–84), Inter Milan (1984–86), Ascoli (1986–87), West Ham United (1987–89)*
Caps: *72 (9 goals)*

An attacking, left-footed midfielder, "Chippy" Brady was the creative playmaker for Arsenal in the 1970s. A relatively slight figure, he had a powerful shot and his passing was immaculate. He made the winning goal in Arsenal's 1979 3–2 FA Cup Final win over Manchester United, and he moved to Juventus in 1980, helping the club to two *Serie A* titles in succession. He played for three other Italian clubs before returning to English football in 1987 with West Ham United. He represented Eire from 1975–90, after which manager Jack Charlton's long–ball style made his stylish midfield play redundant, and he gained 72 Irish caps. After his retirement, he had unsuccessful spells as a manager with Celtic and Brighton. Brady is currently in charge of youth development at Arsenal.

Right: Liam Brady dictating play for Arsenal.

Billy Bremner
(Scotland, 1942–97)

Clubs: *Leeds United (1959–76), Hull City (1976–78) Doncaster Rovers (1978–82)*
Caps: *54 (3 goals)*

The fiery little red-haired Bremner was the midfield motor of Don Revie's Leeds United team in the late 1960s and early 1970s. Bremner's skilful distribution and competitive spirit

Left: Billy Bremner chases the ball for his country in 1973, watched by England's Colin Bell.

helped to bring the club two league titles in 1968–69 and 1973–74, two Fairs Cups in 1968 and 1971, and the 1972 FA Cup, when they beat Arsenal 1–0. He played in the 1975 European Cup Final, when Leeds unluckily lost 2–0 to Bayern Munich, and moved to Hull City soon after. Bremner was first capped in 1965, and he played in the 1974 World Cup, where he missed a chance against Brazil, which would have seen Scotland qualify for the second round. After retiring from the game as a player, he became manager first of Doncaster Rovers and then of Leeds United in the 1980s. Bremner died of a heart attack in 1997.

Emilio Butragueño
(Spain, b. 1963)

Clubs: *Real Madrid (1983–95), Atletico Celaya (1995–98)*
Caps: *69 (26 goals)*

Playing in attack alongside the Mexican Hugo Sanchez, Emilio "The Vulture" Butragueño was Real Madrid's main striker throughout the 1980s. A quick, talented centre-forward, he made his way through the club's youth team, and Real's "nursery" club, Castilla, and his goals brought to the Bernabeu two UEFA Cups, in 1985 and 1986; in both years Butragueño won the *Prix Bravo*

as Europe's best young player. He also helped his Madrid club to five league titles in succession from 1986 to 1990. He made his international debut for Spain against Wales in 1984, scoring in the 3–0 win, and he went on to become Spain's highest-ever goal scorer. His five goals in the 1986 World Cup finals in Mexico made him joint top scorer, and he is particularly remembered for the four goals he collected in Spain's unexpected 5–0 demolition of Denmark in the second round of the tournament.

Right: Butragueño was a Real striker throughout the 1980s.

Above: Manchester United's maestro Eric Cantona takes control of the ball.

Eric Cantona
(France, b. 1966)

Clubs: *Auxerre (1981–88), Marseille (1988–91), Nîmes (1991–92), Leeds United (1992), Manchester United (1992–97)*
Caps: *45 (19 goals)*

Cantona has a complex and volatile personality but is an immensely gifted talent, and his football career has been a rollercoaster ride of unpredictability. His disagreements with clubs and the French international selectors led him to leave France and join Leeds United in early 1992. He spent enough time there to help guide them to the league title but, to the dismay of the Leeds supporters, he moved to Manchester United that summer. With Cantona at the playmaking helm, United won the league four times by 1997, including two "doubles", and Cantona was revered by the Old Trafford fans. His angry Kung Fu kick at a Crystal Palace fan in 1995 brought him notoriety but, after a suspension and a community service order from the courts, he was back at his peak. He was voted Player of the Year in 1996, but he shocked Manchester United at the end of the 1996–97 season by announcing his retirement from football. Cantona is currently carving out an acting career.

Roberto Carlos da Silva (Brazil, b. 1973)

Clubs: *Palmeiras (1993–95), Inter Milan (1995–96), Real Madrid (1996–)*
Caps: *94 (7)*

A stocky, attacking left-back with explosive acceleration, Roberto Carlos is a regular member of the Brazil and Real Madrid teams. He left Palmeiras

Left: Roberto Carlos, Brazilian international and speedy left-back for Real Madrid.

in 1995 to join Inter Milan, but only stayed one season with the Italian club before leaving to join Real. He has since won the Spanish *Liga*, and has three European Cup Winner's medals after Real's 1998, 2000 and 2002 triumphs. Roberto Carlos made his international debut for Brazil in 1992 against the USA, and he played in the 1994 and 1998 World Cup finals. He scored a remarkable 35-yard free-kick in the 1997 Tournoi in France, curving the ball wickedly around the French wall past an astonished goalkeeper. He helped Brazil to World Cup victory as part of the squad in 2002.

Carlos Alberto (Brazil, b. 1944)

Clubs: *Fluminense, Santos, Botafogo, Fluminense, New York Cosmos*
Caps: *53 (8 goals)*

Carlos Alberto stamped his name in footballing history in the 1970 World Cup Final when, as captain and right-back of Brazil, he hammered home an unstoppable right-foot rocket to seal a 4–1 victory for Brazil. A classy and elegant player, he spent his career in Brazil, leaving for the United States in the 1970s to play for New York Cosmos alongside Franz Beckenbauer and Pelé.

Above: Brazil's captain Carlos Alberto cradles the 1970 Jules Rimet trophy.

John Charles (Wales, b. 1931)

Clubs: *Leeds United (1949–57), Juventus (1957–62), Leeds United (1962), Roma (1962–63), Cardiff City (1963–65)*
Caps: *38 (15 goals)*

Although Charles began his Leeds career in 1949 as a centre-half, by the 1956–57 season he had moved to centre-forward and was top scorer in the First Division, with 38 goals.

Left: John Charles rises above the England defence.

A strong, bustling but skilful player, he was bought for his goal-scoring prowess and heading ability by Juventus in 1957, and he became a firm favourite with the Turin crowds who called him the "Gentle Giant". Creating a partnership with the Argentinian inside-forward Omar Sivori, he scored 93 goals in his five seasons with Juventus. He moved back to Leeds for one season in 1962, then moved on to Roma. In his day, he was the youngest player to play for Wales, at the age of 18 years 71 days, and he led his country to the quarter-finals of the 1958 World Cup against Brazil, although injury prevented him playing in that match.

Bobby Charlton (England, b. 1937)

Clubs: *Manchester United (1954–73), Preston North End (1974–75)*
Caps: *106 (49 goals)*

Charlton is one of those rare sportsmen whose name is recognized immediately across the planet, and in his long playing career with Manchester United and England he won virtually all the honours available to a footballer. He made his club debut in 1956, scoring two goals, and was part of the "Busby Babes" side that was virtually destroyed by the Munich air crash in 1958. In the 1960s, with team-mates Denis Law, Pat Crerand and George Best, he helped the club win the FA Cup in 1963, the league in 1967 and the European Cup in 1968, when he scored twice against Benfica in United's 4–1 victory. Initially a left-winger, he moved into the centre of the pitch later in his career, and by the time he retired in 1973, had scored nearly 200 league goals for the club. Internationally, Charlton's finest moment came in 1966 when he was part of the England team that beat

Above: Bobby Charlton moves upfield for Manchester United.

Germany to win the World Cup at Wembley stadium, and he played his last game for England in the 1970 World Cup finals. He was named European Footballer of the Year in 1966, and further honours included the OBE in 1969, the CBE in 1974 and a knighthood in 1994. Bobby Charlton is England's all-time top scorer with 49 goals. He is currently on the board of directors at his old club Manchester United, and is an international ambassador for the FA.

Ray Clemence
(England, b. 1948)

Clubs: *Scunthorpe United (1965–67), Liverpool (1967–81), Tottenham Hotspur (1981–88)*
Caps: *61*

Clemence was an assured, dependable goalkeeper, and would have won many more English caps had it not been for the presence of rival Peter Shilton. Clemence had quick reflexes and sound positioning sense, and he pulled out many fine saves for Liverpool and England. He joined Liverpool from Scunthorpe in 1967, and was the last line of defence in the side that won three European Cups, two UEFA Cups, five league titles and the FA Cup. Seeking a new challenge, he moved to Spurs in 1981 for £300,000 and won an FA Cup medal again in 1982. He made over 250 appearances for the North London club and left in 1988 to become manager of Barnet. Clemence then joined the England national team coaching staff.

Above: Goalkeeper Ray Clemence organizes the Liverpool defence against Manchester United.

Above: Benfica's Mario Coluña (right) shakes hands with Manchester United's Bobby Charlton before the 1968 European Cup final. Manchester won the match.

Mario Coluña
(Mozambique, b. 1935)

Clubs: *Desportivo de Mapotu (1952–54), Benfica (1954–70), Lyons*
Caps: *73 (57 goals)*

Like Eusebio, the other great Mozambique player, Coluña began his career with Desportivo in the capital Mapotu, before moving to Benfica in 1954. Originally a forward with a thunderous left-foot, he was moved to midfield by Benfica's manager Bela Guttmann, and as captain he inspired the great Benfica side of the early 1960s. He scored in Benfica's European Cup Final victories against Barcelona in 1961 and Real Madrid in 1962, and played in three other losing finals that decade. He was captain of Portugal and led his country to third place in the 1966 World Cup. He moved to Lyons before retiring to become Minister of Sport in Mozambique.

Johan Cruyff
(Holland, b. 1947)

Clubs: *Ajax (1964–73), Barcelona (1973–78), Los Angeles Aztecs (1979), Washington Diplomats (1980–81), Levante (1981), Ajax (1981–83), Feyenoord (1983–84)*
Caps: *48 (33 goals)*

Cruyff was the undisputed king of "total football" in the early 1970s. Playing in their free-flowing, fast and exciting style, Cruyff's Ajax won the European Cup three times in succession. He was a graceful, elusive forward with perfect balance and control and an unerring eye for goal, and he was the unselfish inspiration for his gifted team-mates Johan Neeskens and Johnny Rep. He was named European Footballer of the Year in 1971, and in 1972 he scored both goals in Ajax's 2–0 European Cup Final win over Inter Milan. His ex-Ajax manager Rinus Michels persuaded him to join Barcelona in 1973 for £922,000, and in his first season Barça won the Spanish league title. That year, Cruyff captained Holland to the 1974 World Cup Final against West Germany, and his second minute run into the heart of the German defence earned the Dutch a penalty, converted by Neeskens. Germany, however, won the match 2–1. In 1973 and 1974 Cruyff was again voted European Footballer of the Year. He went to the United States in 1978 but came back to Holland in 1981.

Above: Johan Cruyff playing for Holland in the 1974 World Cup finals.

Cruyff launched his coaching career with Ajax in the mid-80s. His lack of formal coaching qualifications did not seem to matter: he led his old club to two further league titles, adding to the six he had won with them as a player. Cruyff returned to Barcelona, as manager, in 1988, and he led the club to their first and only European Cup Final victory, over Sampdoria, in 1992.

Teofilio Cubillas
(Peru, b. 1949)

Clubs: *Alianza, Basle, FC Porto, Fort Lauderdale Strikers*
Caps: *88 (38 goals)*

A predatory striker, Cubillas is probably the finest player ever to have come out of Peru. He made his first international appearance in 1968 against Brazil, and he played in the 1970 and 1978 World Cup finals, scoring five goals in each tournament, as well as appearing in the 1982 finals. He played for his home team Alianza of Lima before moving to Swiss team Basle in 1973, and then had a spell in Portugal with FC Porto. He returned to Alianza in 1977, and ended his career in the United States with Fort Lauderdale Strikers.

Right: Teofilio Cubillas, goal-scoring hero for his country, scored five goals for Peru in both the 1970 and 1978 World Cup finals.

Zoltan Czibor
(Hungary, 1929–1997)

Clubs: *Ferencvaros, Csepel, Honved, Barcelona, Espanyol*
Caps: *43 (17 goals)*

One of the "Magnificent Magyars" of the 1950s, along with Ferenc Puskas, Sandor Kocsis and Ladislav Kubala, Zoltan Czibor was a left-winger with a powerful shot. He left Hungary after the 1956 revolution and moved to Spain, where he signed for Barcelona –

Left: Zoltan Czibor (right) contests possession for Hungary.

along with his Honved team-mate Kocsis. Czibor won the Spanish league title twice with Barcelona, and he scored two goals in their 1960 Fairs Cup defeat of Birmingham. He also scored in the 1961 European Cup Final when Barcelona, unluckily, lost 3–2 to Benfica. He ended his playing career with a short spell at neighbouring Spanish club Espanyol. Czibor's international career for Hungary was limited and he only played in the 1954 World Cup Final, where the East Europeans were defeated 3–2 by West Germany. After retiring from professional football, Czibor returned to Hungary. He died there in 1997.

Kenny Dalglish
(Scotland, b. 1951)

Clubs: *Celtic (1966–77), Liverpool (1977–89)*
Caps: *102 (30 goals)*

Dalglish was a young Rangers supporter who became the darling of Celtic Park. A tenacious inside-forward with a deadly shot, he had immaculate ball control and could pass the ball in the tightest of defensive situations. While at Celtic he won four league titles and four Scottish Cups, but in 1977 he moved to Liverpool, as a replacement for Kevin Keegan, in a record £440,000 deal. He scored the winner in the 1978 European Cup Final against Bruges with a delicate chip over the keeper, and soon became the creative heart of Bob Paisley's side. In his Anfield career he won two more European Cups and six league winner's medals. First capped in 1971, he went on to collect a record 102 Scottish caps, including the World Cups of 1974, 1978 and 1982. He shares with Denis Law the record for the most goals scored (30) for Scotland. He became player-manager of Liverpool the day after the Heysel disaster of 1985, and later left to become manager of Blackburn Rovers and Newcastle United. Dalglish was appointed Director of Football with Celtic in 1999 but resigned in 2000.

Above: "King Kenny" Dalglish on the attack for Scotland against England.

Edgar Davids
(Surinam, b. 1973)

Clubs: *Ajax (1991–96), AC Milan (1996–97), Juventus (1997–)*
Caps: *53 (6 goals)*

Davids is a tough little competitor who tenaciously controls the Juventus midfield. Known as "pitbull" by his team-mates because of his aggression and lack of fear, Davids is a clever passer of the ball and can unleash a ferocious shot. Easily identified by the specially made eyeglasses he sometimes wears for glaucoma (which he needed permission from FIFA to wear during matches), Davids is one of the many top European players who came up through the Ajax youth team, making his first team debut in 1991, at the age of 18. He won the European Cup with Ajax in 1995 and acquired three league title winner's medals before departing for AC Milan in 1996. He moved on to Juventus in 1997. An outspoken individual, Davids was sent home from Euro '96 after an argument with Dutch coach Gus Hiddink. It was Davids' last-minute, long-range goal that squeezed Holland past Yugoslavia into the 1998 World Cup quarter-final.

Right: Edgar Davids in full flight.

Alessandro Del Piero
(Italy, b. 1974)

Clubs: *Padova (1990–93), Juventus (1993–)*
Caps: *55 (20 goals)*

Likened early in his career to the young Roberto Baggio, Del Piero is a forward of genius. A right-footed player who is particularly effective in the inside-left position, he is fast, difficult to dispossess and can shimmy his way through packed defences to score some excellent goals. Del Piero moved from Padova to Juventus in 1993, and he scored a hat trick in his third game for the Turin club, against Parma. He is particularly dangerous from the dead ball, and his goals have helped Juventus to win three *Serie A* league titles. In the 1997–98 season he scored 21 league goals for Juve, as well as a hat trick against Monaco in the semi-final of the European Cup, which took the Italian side into the final. Del Piero is prone to injury and he badly damaged his knee in late 1998 but, when fit, there are few more skilful forwards in European football today. He played for Italy in the World Cup finals of 1998 and 2002.

Left: Juve's forward Alessandro Del Piero representing Italy against Brazil.

Kazimierz Deyna
(Poland, 1947–1989)

Clubs: *Starogard, Sportowy (KS) Lodz, Legia Warsaw, Manchester City, San Diego*
Caps: *102 (38 goals)*

Deyna was the midfield supremo of the Polish side that included Kasperczak, Lato and Gadocha, and it was his skill in the centre that resulted in Poland's success on the world footballing stage during the 1970s. A natural attacking player, Deyna helped the national side take the gold medal in the 1972 Munich Olympics (where he scored two goals in the final and a total of nine in the tournament), and to its best-ever result of third place in the World Cup finals of 1974. Deyna died in a car crash in the United States in 1989.

Right: Kazimierz Deyna (left) sets up a Polish attacking move.

Didi, Waldir Pereira
(Brazil, 1928–2001)

Clubs: *Rio Branco, Lencoes, Madureiro, Fluminense, Botafogo, Real Madrid, Valéncia, Botafogo*
Caps: *85 (31 goals)*

The midfield maestro of the Brazilian sides of the 1950s, and a master of the spot-kick, Didi played in the 1954 World Cup finals, where he scored two goals. He was at the heart of the 1958 Brazilian team that introduced the 4–2–4 formation and won that year's World Cup Final, playing with the young Pelé, Vava and Zagallo. He played again in the 1962 tournament. He left South America for Real Madrid in 1959, but his playing style did not fit in with Di Stefano, and he left Madrid for Valéncia, before moving back to Botafogo. On retiring, Didi became manager of the Peruvian national team. He died in 2001.

Left: Didi, Brazil's celebrated playmaker during the 1950s.

Alfredo Di Stefano (Argentina, b. 1926)

Clubs: *River Plate (1943–49), Millionaros Bogotá (1949–53), Real Madrid (1953–64), Espanyol (1964–66)*
Caps: *7 (7 goals) (Argentina), 2 (Colombia), 31 (23 goals) (Spain)*

For many, the greatest all-round footballer in the history of the game, Di Stefano alternated between midfield and attack, plundering goals and creating chances for his illustrious Real Madrid team-mates. He was at the centre of the magnificent Real side that won the European Cup five times running from 1956–60, and his partnership with Ferenc Puskas devastated defences throughout Europe. In his first game for Real, in 1953, he put four goals past Barcelona, and his arrival sparked off a revival in the fortunes of the Spanish side. Di Stefano scored in every European Cup Final from 1956–60, culminating in a hat trick against Eintracht Frankfurt in 1960, and played on the losing side in two more finals, in 1962 and 1964.

He scored 49 goals in his 56 games in the tournament, which is a record that still stands today. He collected eight Spanish league winner's medals with the club and was named European Footballer of the Year in 1957 and 1959. After the 1964 European Cup Final he moved to Espanyol. He retired as a player in 1966, but went on to manage Boca Juniors, Sporting Lisbon, River Plate, Valéncia and Real Madrid.

Below: The incomparable Alfredo Di Stefano on the attack for Real Madrid.

William "Dixie" Dean
(England, 1907–1980)

Clubs: *Tranmere Rovers (1924–25), Everton (1925–38), Notts County (1938), Sligo Rovers (1939)*
Caps: *16 (18 goals)*

Dean was a goal scorer extraordinaire and in the 1927–28 season, at the age of 21, he set a record, which still stands today, of 60 league goals in just one season. Dean was of medium height and build but he had a prodigious

Left: William "Dixie" Dean, Everton's great pre-war striker.

heading ability, and he was a strong, two-footed player. He moved to Everton from Tranmere Rovers in 1925, and scored seven hat tricks in his record-breaking season, which helped to win Everton the league title. In 1931–32 he scored 44 goals, and Everton again claimed the league title. He moved to Nottingham County in 1938, and then to Ireland's Sligo Rovers, and retired in 1939, having scored an outstanding 379 goals in 438 league games and 28 goals in 33 Cup ties. He scored 18 goals in his 16 international appearances for England. Dixie died in 1980 while watching an Everton game at Goodison Park.

Dragan Dzajic
(Yugoslavia, b. 1946)

Clubs: *Red Star Belgrade, Bastia, Red Star Belgrade*
Caps: *85 (23 goals)*

Dzajic, nicknamed the "Magic Dragan" by the English newspapers, was a fast, intelligent outside-left; he maintained his pace throughout his career, and was still being selected to play as outside-left in his later years. Dzajic was the most-capped player in the former Yugoslavia. He won five league

titles and four Yugoslavian cups with Red Star Belgrade, and he scored 23 goals in 85 games for his country. Dzajic is best remembered in England for the 1968 European Championships, when he scored the goal, with four minutes to go, which eliminated England in the semi-final. He scored again in the final of that tournament, but Italy equalized and went on to win. Dzajic retired as a player in 1978, and became manager of Red Star.

Right: Dragan Dzajic (right) playing for Yugoslavia.

Duncan Edwards
(England, 1936–1958)

Clubs: *Manchester United (1952–58)*
Caps: *18 (5 goals)*

With the potential to have been one of England's greatest all-round footballers, the powerful and skilful Edwards was one the "Babes" of Matt Busby's Manchester United team of the 1950s, and, tragically, he was one of the victims of the Munich air crash of 1958. Although a big man, he had pace

Left: Duncan Edwards in one of his all-too-few appearances for England.

and subtlety, and his thunderous shot – for which he was given the nickname "Boom-Boom" – brought him several important goals for his club and country. He made his club debut for Manchester United at the age of 16, and he gained the first of his 18 international caps in a 7–2 victory against Scotland two years later, aged 18. He was England's youngest-ever full international, and rated by Matt Busby "the most complete footballer in Britain – if not the world". In his brief career he made 175 appearances for Manchester United, and he helped the club to two league titles, in 1956 and 1957. Edwards' untimely death in Munich robbed England and United of a massively gifted talent.

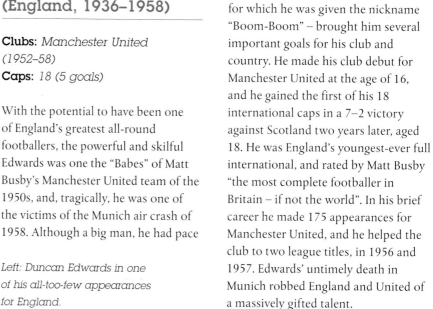

Stefan Effenberg
(Germany, b. 1968)

Clubs: *Borussia Mönchengladbach (1987–90), Bayern Munich (1990–92), Fiorentina (1992–94), Borussia Mönchengladbach (1994–98), Bayern Munich (1998–)*
Caps: *35 (5 goals)*

A tall, fair-haired midfielder, Stefan Effenberg began his career with Borussia Mönchengladbach, winning the *Bundesliga* title in 1990. He moved to Bayern Munich the following season, and then spent two years in Italy with Fiorentina. He returned to Mönchengladbach in 1994 and won a German Cup medal with them in 1995. He is currently playing for Bayern, with whom he won more league titles in 1999 and 2000. He was first capped in 1991, for a game against Wales, and was included in Germany's 1994 World Cup squad. He led Bayern to victory in the 2001 European Cup.

Right: The combative Stefan Effenberg.

Eusebio da Silva Ferreira
(Mozambique, b. 1942)

Clubs: *Sporting Club of Lourenço Marques (1958–61), Benfica (1961–75)*
Caps: *64 (41 goals)*

Eusebio, the "Black Pearl", played his first game for Bela Guttmann's Benfica in 1961. By the end of that season he had won a European Cup winner's medal, with his two goals against Real Madrid helping Benfica to a 5–3 victory. He scored again in the 1963 final, but this time his team was beaten by two goals from AC Milan's José Altafini. He played in two more finals, in 1965 against Inter Milan and in 1968 against Manchester United, but was on the losing side both times; in the latter match only a fine save from goalkeeper Alex Stepney stopped Eusebio from scoring a winner. Eusebio's trademark right-footed shot brought him the Portuguese top scorer award in seven seasons and, by the time he moved to play in North America in 1975, he had collected ten Portuguese league winner's medals. He was named European Footballer of the Year in 1965. He made his debut for Portugal in 1961 (he was entitled to pay for Portugal as a national of Mozambique, one of its colonies), and was top scorer in the 1966 World Cup with nine goals, four in one game. In 1977, Eusebio returned to Benfica as coach.

Left: Eusebio powers his way to goal.

Above: Italy's Giacinto Facchetti (right) in the 1970 World Cup Final against Brazil.

Giacinto Facchetti
(Italy, b. 1942)

Clubs: *Trevigliese (1956–60), Inter Milan (1960–78)*
Caps: *94 (3 goals)*

Facchetti was a tall, elegant, attacking left-back at the heart of Helenio Hererra's *catenaccio* system at Inter Milan in the 1960s. He joined Inter in 1960 and won four league titles with the Milanese side in his time at the San Siro. He collected two European Cup medals in 1964 and 1965, and scored the brilliant goal that eliminated Liverpool in the semi-final of the 1965 European Cup. He made his international debut in 1963 against Turkey, and was appointed captain in 1966, the year in which he scored ten goals in the *Serie A*. He captained Italy to the final against Brazil in the World Cup of 1970, and he played again in 1974 as a sweeper. He missed the 1978 World Cup through injury.

Giovanni Ferrari
(Italy, 1907–1982)

Clubs: *Alessandria, Juventus, Ambrosiana (Inter Milan), Bologna*
Caps: *44 (14 goals)*

Ferrari was an inside-forward with Vittorio Pozzo's remarkable and successful Italian team of the 1930s. He played in the 1934 World Cup Final team that beat Czechoslovakia 2–1 in extra time. With Giuseppe Meazza, he played again in the 1938 World Cup Final, when Italy beat Hungary 4–2. Ferrari won the Italian league title five times with Juventus, and in 1940 he joined Inter Milan (at that time called Ambrosiana) and took the league medal again. He ended his playing career with Bologna. He managed Italy for the 1962 World Cup, and was in charge for the infamous "Battle of Santiago", when Italy and Chile punched and kicked their way through a first-round match.

Above: Ferrari (in front of man with hat) and the 1938 Italian World Cup team.

Luis Figo
(Portugal, b. 1972)

Clubs: *Sporting Lisbon (1989–95),*
Barcelona (1995–2000),
Real Madrid (2000–)
Caps: *88 (27 goals)*

A powerful winger with skill and stamina, Figo is currently one of the finest forwards in European football. A goal provider and a scorer, and able to play on either wing, he was outstanding in the Barcelona attack. He made his debut with Sporting Lisbon at 17 and left the club in 1995. He was pursued by Parma and Juventus, but a confusion over contracts saw him banned from Italian football for two years and he was snapped up by Barcelona for £1.5 million. After success at Euro 2000, Figo was bought by Real Madrid that summer for £37 million. He was European Footballer of the Year in 2000, and World Footballer of the Year in 2001.

Above: Luis Figo, star of Euro 2000 and 2001 World Footballer of the Year, but disappointing at the 2002 World Cup.

Tom Finney
(England, b. 1922)

Club: *Preston North End (1936–60)*
Caps: *76 (30 goals)*

Tom Finney was one of England's most versatile players in the years after World War Two. Although a conventional winger, he was tough in the tackle, two-footed and could score goals. He spent his career with Preston North End and never won any major domestic honours, but internationally he gained 76 caps and played in every forward position for his country. Finney made his debut for Preston in 1936 and for England in 1946. He played in the World Cups finals of 1950, 1954 and 1958, and won his last England cap in 1959. Finney retired in 1960. He was twice voted Footballer of the Year, in 1954 and 1957, and was knighted in 1997. Finney was never booked or sent off in his entire career, though he played almost 500 games for Preston, where he became club president.

Above: The flying Tom Finney, one of England's finest-ever wingers.

Just Fontaine
(Morocco, b. 1933)

Clubs: *AC Marrakesh, USM Casablanca (1950–53), Nice (1953–56), Reims (1956–62)*
Caps: *21 (30 goals)*

A small, strong striker with sharp acceleration and lightening reflexes, Fontaine led the French national attack in the second half of the 1950s. He joined Nice in 1953 and was bought by Reims in 1956 to replace Raymond Kopa, who was on his way to Real Madrid. In 1958 he helped Reims to the French "double". His entry on to the international scene, and his first

Left: Just Fontaine on the attack for France.

cap for France, came in 1958, when he was called up to replace René Bliard, who had been injured on the eve of the World Cup finals. Fontaine scored a still-unbeaten record of 13 goals in the tournament that year (although much credit is owed to his team-mate Kopa, for creating the chances), in Sweden, and France reached third place in the tournament. Fontaine played in the 1959 European Cup Final, when Reims lost to Real Madrid but, in 1960, with Kopa now back at the club and the creative partnership between him and Fontaine again in evidence, Reims won the league. A double fracture of his leg ended his career prematurely in 1962. Later, Fontaine was president of the French player's union, and for a short time, in 1967, he took over the role of director of the French national team.

Paulo Futre
(Portugal, b. 1966)

Clubs: *Sporting Lisbon (1978–84), FC Porto (1984–87), Atlético Madrid (1987–92), Benfica (1992–93), Marseille (1993), Reggiana (1993–95), AC Milan (1995–96), West Ham United (1996), Atlético Madrid (1997–2002)*
Caps: *41 (6 goals)*

The much-travelled winger Futre was a teenage prodigy with Sporting Lisbon and Portugal, and he made his international debut at the age of 17. He moved to Porto, and his attacking link with the Algerian forward Madjer helped bring Porto their only European Cup, when they beat Bayern Munich 2–1 in 1987. Futre left soon afterwards to join first Atlético Madrid and then Benfica, in 1993. Marseille bought him but sold him within a few months to *Serie A* side Reggiana for £8 million. He moved to AC Milan, and had a season with West Ham United, before returning to Atlético in the late 1990s.

Right: Paulo Futre playing for Porto in the club's triumphant European Cup Final of 1987.

Garrincha, Manuel Francisco dos Santos (Brazil, 1933–1983)

Clubs: *Pau Grande (1947–53), Botafogo (1953–66), Corinthians, Barranquilla Flamengo, Red Star Paris, Portugesa, Olaria*
Caps: *50 (13 goals)*

A small man with legs deformed by childhood polio, Garrincha, meaning "songbird", was nonetheless one of the greatest wingers of all time. He had electric pace, and was a dazzlingly effective dribbler with a powerful shot.

He created the first two goals in the 1958 World Cup Final, won 5–2 by Brazil, and he played again in the 1962 tournament. With Pelé unfit, Garrincha took over as centre-forward and scored two goals in the quarter-final against England, and another two in the semi-final against Chile. He collected his second World Cup winner's medal that year when Brazil beat Czechoslovakia 3–1. In the 1966 World Cup, an unfit Garrincha could not prevent his side's elimination in the first round. He died from the effects of alcoholism in 1983.

Right: Garrincha (left) takes on Sweden.

Above: Paul Gascoigne in England's win over Scotland in Euro '96.

Paul Gascoigne (England, b. 1967)

Clubs: *Newcastle United (1985–88), Tottenham Hotspur (1988–92), Lazio (1992–95), Rangers (1995–98), Middlesbrough (1998–2000), Everton (2000–2), Burnley (2002), Gansu Tianma (2003–)*
Caps: *57 (10 goals)*

Paul Gascoigne is overweight, prone to childish antics and unpredictable, but at his best he was one of England's greatest ever midfielders. Strong, with a delicate touch, his passing and dribbling abilities were peerless, and he packed a powerful shot. Bought as a young lad by Terry Venables from Newcastle in 1988, he helped Spurs to reach the 1991 FA Cup Final, where he badly injured his leg in a rash tackle. He moved to Lazio the following year but could not settle, and Glasgow Rangers bought him in 1995. His 14 goals helped Rangers win the Scottish league in 1995–6, when "Gazza" was voted Scottish Footballer of the Year. He got his first cap in 1988 and had a memorable World Cup in 1990, ending with the famous tears when England lost to West Germany in the semi-final. He scored the goal of the tournament in Euro '96 to put England 2–0 ahead against Scotland, but his international career was terminated in 1998 by Glenn Hoddle. Gascoigne currently plays in China.

Claudio Gentile
(Libya, b. 1953)

Clubs: *Arona, Varese, Juventus, Fiorentina*
Caps: *71 (1 goal)*

A tough, notoriously hard-tackling right-back, Gentile was the perfect foil for skilful sweeper Gaetano Scirea at Juventus and in the Italian national team. He helped Juventus to win six *Serie A* titles and two Italian Cups between 1977 and 1986, and he also played in the club's 1977 UEFA Cup and 1984 Cup Winners' Cup triumphs. He played in the 1978 World Cup finals, and was one of the six Juventus players who represented Italy in 1982 to win the World Cup trophy.

Left: Italy's Claudio Gentile (left) takes on Argentina's Diego Maradona.

Francisco Paco Gento
(Spain, b. 1933)

Clubs: *Santander (1950–53), Real Madrid (1953–70)*
Caps: *43 (5 goals)*

Gento was a fast, skilful outside-left for Real Madrid when the Spanish club ruled European football. He was arch-supplier to the deadly Alfredo Di Stefano and Ferenc Puskas in the side that won the European Cup for five successive years, from 1956–60. Gento played in eight European Cup finals, winning six of them, and he scored the extra-time winner in 1958, when Real Madrid beat AC Milan 3–2. He was Real's captain in their 1964 3–1 defeat by Inter Milan, and again in their 1966 2–1 win over Partizan Belgrade. In total, this great club servant made nearly 800 appearances for Real, and he helped the club to 12 Spanish league titles between 1954 and 1969.

Right: Winger Paco Gento in the all-white strip of Real Madrid.

Ryan Giggs
(Wales, b. 1973)

Clubs: *Manchester United (1991–)*
Caps: *40 (7 goals)*

Cardiff-born Giggs signed for Manchester United in 1990 and made his league debut for the club in 1991. A strong and speedy left-winger with an eye for goal, he quickly became a first-team regular and he has since gained a host of honours with the club, including a European Cup winner's medal in 1999. Giggs has scored many important goals for United, but probably none as impressive as the goal against Arsenal in the 1999 FA Cup semi-final, when he ran almost half the length of the pitch, evading tackles to score the winner with a rasping shot in extra time. Gaining his first cap at the age of 17 years and 332 days, Giggs beat John Charles' record to be the youngest player to represent Wales, although he has since lost that title to the young Welsh international Ryan Green.

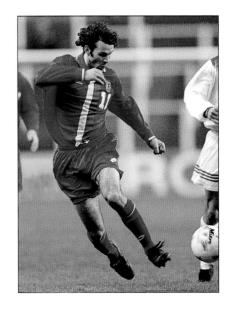

Right: Ryan Giggs speeds towards goal for Wales against Turkey.

Johnny Giles
(Ireland, b. 1940)

Clubs: *Manchester United (1957–63), Leeds United (1963–75), West Bromwich Albion (1975–77), Shamrock Rovers (1977–80)*
Caps: *59 (5 goals)*

A gifted midfield player, with a strong shot and a precise ability to find a team-mate with a short or long ball, Giles began his career on the right wing with Manchester United. He won an FA Cup winner's medal with the club in 1962 and transferred to Leeds United in 1963. He moved to midfield and, with his partner Billy Bremner, formed the creative engine of Don Revie's team. His skill was matched by an uncompromising determination, and he drove on Leeds to win two Fairs Cups, in 1966 and 1968, and two league titles, as well as playing in the 1975 European Cup Final, when the club were beaten 2–0 by Bayern Munich. This disappointment was Giles' last appearance for Leeds. He moved first to West Bromwich Albion as player-manager, and then to Shamrock Rovers in the same role. He was the youngest-ever player to represent Ireland, and he played his last international game in 1979.

Left: Johnny Giles (right) rises to the occasion for Leeds United.

Above: Greaves, Spurs' prolific goal scorer, playing for the club against Everton.

Jimmy Greaves
(England, b. 1940)

Clubs: *Chelsea (1957–61), AC Milan (1961), Tottenham Hotspur (1961–70), West Ham United (1970–71)*
Caps: *57 (44 goals)*

A cool, devastatingly effective striker with close control and mesmerizing dribbling skills, Greaves was the finest goal scorer of his generation. By the age of 20 he had scored 100 goals for Chelsea. He moved to AC Milan in 1961, but after only ten league games for the Italian club he joined Spurs for £99,999 (to avoid being Britain's first £100,000 player). In his nine years at White Hart Lane he was top scorer in the First Division six times. Greaves gained his first international cap in 1959, scoring against Peru, and in 1961 he scored 11 times in five internationals, including a hat trick in England's 9–3 hammering of Scotland. He played in the 1962 World Cup finals and in three of England's matches in the 1966 finals, but he was not selected for the final itself. A deeply disappointed Greaves never played for England again. His total of 44 international goals places him just behind Bobby Charlton and Gary Lineker in the scoring stakes. On his retirement, he endured a period of alcoholism but came back as a popular newspaper and TV pundit.

Gunnar Gren
(Sweden, 1920–1991)

Clubs: *IFK Gothenburg, AC Milan (1949–53), Fiorentina (1953–55), Genoa (1955–56), GAIS Gothenburg (1956–59)*
Caps: *57 (32 goals)*

Known as "The Professor" because of both his premature baldness and his intelligent play, Gren was an astute inside-forward who began his career with IFK Gothenburg. He played for Sweden in the 1948 Olympic Games, helping the team to win a gold medal in the final against Yugoslavia, and he moved to AC Milan in 1949, where he teamed up with fellow Swedes Gunnar Nordahl and Nils Liedholm to form the famed "Gre-no-li" attack. Gren helped Milan to the *Serie A* title in 1951 before returning to Sweden in 1956. He played again for his country, in what was to be the last of his international games, in the 1958 World Cup Final. Although Sweden were the first to score, they were deservedly beaten 5–2 by Pelé and Brazil. Gunnar Gren died in 1991.

Above: "The Professor", Gunnar Gren.

Ruud Gullit
(Holland, b. 1962)

Clubs: *Haarlem (1979–82), Feyenoord (1982–85), PSV Eindhoven (1985–87), AC Milan (1987–93), AC Milan (1994), Sampdoria (1994–95), Chelsea (1995–98)*
Caps: *65 (16 goals)*

A tall, athletic player with surprisingly delicate touch and control, Gullit was the inspiration behind the success of AC Milan and Holland in the late 1980s and early 1990s. Bought by Milan in 1987 from PSV Eindhoven for a record £6 million, Gullit led the Italian side to successive European Cup victories in 1989 and 1990. He played in the 1994 final, in Milan's 4–0 humbling of Barcelona, but moved soon afterwards to Sampdoria then Chelsea, taking over as player-manager in 1997. He left in 1998 to manage Newcastle United for a year. Internationally, he was capped in 1981 and his Dutch side won the European Championships in 1988. He played in the 1990 World Cup but did not appear in 1994, an argument with Dutch coach Advocaat prompting his walkout.

Right: Ruud Gullit leaves Denmark's John Jensen on the ground in the 1992 European Championship.

Gheorghe Hagi
(Romania, b. 1965)

Clubs: *Sportul Studentesc (1982–86), Steaua Bucharest (1986–90), Real Madrid (1990–92), Brescia (1992–94), Barcelona (1994–96), Galatasaray (1996–2002)*
Caps: *125 (34 goals)*

Romania's most-capped player, Hagi is a single-minded striker who gained his first cap at 18. In 1986 he joined Steaua Bucharest, and his scoring prowess propelled them to three league titles in

Left: Romania's greatest footballer, Hagi.

succession, and to the 1989 European Cup Final, where an unusually quiescent Steaua lost 4–0 to AC Milan. Known as the "Maradona of the Carpathians", Hagi moved to Real Madrid in 1990, and to Brescia in 1992. He joined Cruyff's Barcelona in 1994 but did not play to his potential. Hagi's last club was Galatasaray, with whom he won the UEFA Cup Final in 2000. He has played in three World Cup finals. In 1990 his Romanian side were eliminated on penalties by Ireland in the second round; in 1994 they made the quarter-final stage before being knocked out by Sweden; and in 1998 they lost to Croatia in the second round.

Kurt Hamrin
(Sweden, b. 1934)

Clubs: *AIK (1952–56), Juventus (1956–57), Padova (1957–58), Fiorentina (1958–67), AC Milan (1967–69), Napoli (1969–71)*
Caps: *32 (16 goals)*

A fast goal-scoring right-winger, Hamrin's goals helped Fiorentina to the 1961 European Cup Winners Cup: his goal, four minutes from time in the second leg killed off Rangers' hopes of taking the trophy. He had played for Juventus before joining Fiorentina, but he quickly adjusted to Italian football. Later, at AC Milan, he played in the side that beat Ajax in the 1969 European Cup Final. He ended his career with Napoli and then Caserta. He played for Sweden in the 1958 World Cup.

Above: Sweden's Kurt Hamrin played most of his club football in Italy.

Above: Liverpool's cultured defender Alan Hansen.

Alan Hansen
(Scotland, b. 1955)

Clubs: *Partick Thistle (1973–77), Liverpool (1977–90)*
Caps: *22*

A tall, cultured and elegant central defender, Hansen was a member of the team that brought Liverpool so much silverware in the 1970s and 1980s. He joined from Partick Thistle in 1977 for £100,000, and by the time he retired in 1990, he had won eight league titles, two FA Cups and three European Cups. He played over 600 games for Liverpool, captained the club to the "double" in 1986, and his calm authority and vision were crucial to the Reds' success. He played 22 times for Scotland, and appeared in the 1982 World Cup finals but was dropped for the 1986 tournament. He became a television commentator with the BBC, and made the famous proclamation, when discussing the prospects of the young Manchester United side, that "you can't win anything with kids." Alex Ferguson's team promptly went on to win the English "double".

Ernest Happel
(Austria, 1925–1992)

Clubs: *Rapid Vienna, First Vienna, Racing Club de Paris*
Caps: *51 (5 goals)*

Happel was a tough, skilful centre-half with Rapid Vienna in the 1950s. He was renowned for the ferocity of his shot from a dead ball, and he scored a hat trick against Real Madrid in a European Cup match in 1957. He played for the celebrated Austrian national side in both the 1954 and 1958 World Cup finals, and became a successful manager on his retirement. He managed Feyenoord to their only European Cup triumph in 1970, beating Celtic 2–1 by playing an early brand of "total football". He also guided Hamburg to their European Cup Final 1–0 victory over Juventus in 1983, and led Bruges to their 1–0 1978 final defeat by Liverpool. He succeeded Rinus Michels as coach to the Dutch national team, and led them all the way to the 1978 World Cup Final. Happel died of cancer in 1992, and the Prater stadium in Vienna was renamed the Ernest Happel-Stadion in his honour.

Right: Ernest Happel lines up with the FIFA World X1 squad in 1953.

Johnny Haynes
(England, b. 1934)

Clubs: *Fulham (1952–69)*
Caps: *56 (18 goals)*

Although Haynes was one of the sweetest passers of a ball that England has ever seen, he never won a trophy with his only club, Fulham. He made his debut in 1952, and by the end of the decade had become a massive influence on the game. As well as his uncanny distribution skills, he was a frequent goal scorer, and he effortlessly dictated the pace and direction of play. Haynes was the first £100-a-week footballer, on the abolition of the maximum wage in 1961, and he captained England from 1959–62, until a bad car accident led to his retirement from international football. In that period, he led England to their 1961 9–3 defeat of Scotland, scoring twice, and to the country's ill-fated 1962 World Cup finals in Chile. He left Fulham in 1969 to become player-manager with South Africa's Durban City, returning to live in retirement in Scotland.

Left: Fulham and England captain, Johnny Haynes.

Nandor Hidegkuti
(Hungary, 1922–2000)

Clubs: *MTK Budapest*
(then known as Voros Lobogo)
(1938–58)
Caps: *68 (39 goals)*

Hidegkuti was one of the "Magnificent Magyars", the great Hungarian team of the 1950s. He pioneered the role of the deep-lying centre-forward, when he would lurk behind his forwards and

Left: Hungarian deep-lying centre-forward Nandor Hidegkuti.

burst through to score past the bemused defence. He used the ploy to devastating effect when he scored within the first minute, and plundered two more, in Hungary's 6–3 defeat of England in 1953; he played it again in the 7–1 rout against England in Budapest six months later. Hidegkuti was in the team that took the gold medal at the 1952 Olympics, and he also played in the 1954 World Cup Final, where an unlucky Hungary lost 3–2 to West Germany. Hidegkuti also played in the World Cup finals in 1958. On his retirement, Hidegkuti became coach of Vasas and then Fiorentina.

Glenn Hoddle
(England, b. 1957)

Clubs: *Tottenham Hotspur (1975–87), Monaco (1987–91), Swindon Town (1991–93), Chelsea (1993–95)*
Caps: *53 (8 goals)*

A creative midfield player with exceptional touch, control and a powerful shot, Hoddle was the hero of White Hart Lane in the early 1980s. He could be inconsistent but, on form, he was unstoppable. Hoddle won two FA Cup medals, in 1981 and 1982, scoring in the latter and in the replay against Queen's Park Rangers. He also claimed his UEFA Cup medal in 1984, when Spurs defeated Anderlecht on penalties. After Spurs lost the 1987 FA Cup Final, Hoddle moved to Arsène Wenger's Monaco. He first represented his country in 1979, scoring against Bulgaria on his debut, and he played in the 1982 and 1986 World Cup finals. He moved back to England, in 1991, to become player-manager of Swindon Town, and he later performed the same role at Chelsea. He coached England from 1996 to 1999, and was appointed manager of Tottenham Hotspur in 2001.

Right: Spurs' hero Glenn Hoddle sets up another sweet pass.

Jairzinho, Jair Ventura Filho (Brazil, b. 1944)

Clubs: *Botafogo (1959–71), Marseille (1971–73), Cruzeiro (1973–76), Portuguesa (1976–78)*
Caps: *82 (34 goals)*

The natural heir to Garrincha in the Brazilian national team, Jairzinho was a speedy, goal-scoring right-winger. He was capped in 1963. Despite a serious injury in 1967, he played in the 1970 World Cup finals, where he set a record by scoring in every round, including Brazil's third goal when he converted a header from Pelé in the 4–1 final win over Italy. He moved to Marseille for a brief, unsettled spell, and returned to Brazil with Cruzeiro, helping the club to win the *Copa Libertadores* championship in 1976. He ended his career with Venezuela's Portuguesa. Jairzinho is credited with discovering the young Ronaldo in the early 1990s.

Above: Jairzinho, Brazil's goal-scoring star of the 1970 World Cup finals in Mexico.

Above: Alex James, the creative hub of Arsenal's 1930s side.

Alex James (Scotland, 1901–53)

Clubs: *Raith Rovers (1922–25), Preston North End (1925–29), Arsenal (1929–37)*
Caps: *8 (4 goals)*

James was a short, aggressive inside-forward with marvellous ball skills and passing ability. He was Preston's leading goal scorer before he was bought by Herbert Chapman, in 1929; he added the final creative touch to the Arsenal team that dominated the 1930s playing their new "WM" formation. He was chief schemer and supplier to the Arsenal attack featuring Lambert, Jack and Bastin, which brought the club four league titles from 1930 to 1935, as well as two FA Cups in 1930 and 1936. He played for Scotland on only a few occasions, but he was a member of the "Wembley Wizards" side, which convincingly beat England 5–1 in 1928. James retired from football in 1937. He died from cancer in 1953.

Pat Jennings
(N. Ireland, b. 1945)

Clubs: *Newry Town (1961–63), Watford (1963–64), Tottenham Hotspur (1964–77), Arsenal (1977–85)*
Caps: *119*

A gentle giant of a goalkeeper, the dependable Jennings joined Spurs from Watford for £27,000 in 1964, when he also made his international debut. In his time at Spurs, he made nearly 450 league appearances for the club,

Left: Pat Jennings clutches the ball in his massive hands.

breaking the club's existing appearance record, and collected an FA Cup and a UEFA Cup winner's medal. Jennings also became Northern Ireland's most capped player. When Spurs were relegated in 1977, Jennings moved down the road to join Arsenal, for whom he played until 1985 (making way for John Lukic when he left). He won another FA Cup winner's medal in Arsenal's 3–2 defeat of Manchester United in 1979. He played for Northern Ireland in the 1982 and 1986 World Cup finals, retiring after their defeat by Brazil. Jennings once scored direct from a goal-kick, in a Charity Shield match against Manchester United in 1967.

Jimmy Johnstone
(Scotland, b. 1944)

Clubs: *Celtic (1961–75), San José Earthquakes (1975), Sheffield United (1975), Dundee (1977)*
Caps: *23 (4 goals)*

"Jinky" Johnstone rose from being a ballboy at Parkhead in the 1950s to become one of Celtic's and Scotland's greatest-ever players, making his international debut in 1964. A small, ginger-haired right-winger, Johnstone was master of the dribble, a fine crosser of the ball and an expert finisher. He was central to Jock Stein's memorable side of the 1960s and 1970s, when Celtic won the Scottish League title nine times in a row, collected seven Scottish Cups and famously became the first British winners of the European Cup in 1967. Johnstone was often at his best in European competitions, and he relished the opportunity to demonstrate his skills on the wider stage. However, he was marked out of the game in Celtic's 2–1 defeat by Feyenoord in the 1970 European Cup Final. He left Celtic in 1975.

Right: Jimmy Johnstone sets off on another dribble for Celtic.

Nwankwo Kanu
(Nigeria, b. 1976)

Clubs: *Federated Works (1991–92), Iwanyanu (1992–93), Ajax (1993–96), Inter Milan (1996–98), Arsenal (1998–)*
Caps: *37 (6 goals)*

Nigerian striker Kanu was 18 when he joined Ajax in 1993. The lanky player immediately settled in and helped Ajax win three Dutch league titles in succession from 1994 to 1996. He also came on as a substitute in Ajax's European Cup Final win over AC Milan in 1995, and played in the 1996 defeat by Juventus. A serious heart valve condition threatened to end his career, but following corrective surgery, Kanu joined Arsenal in 1998. He has scored some memorable goals in his time with them, including a winning hat trick in ten minutes against Chelsea, and a superb long-range back-heel against Middlesbrough. He represented Nigeria in the 1996 Olympic Games when they beat first Brazil in the semi-final (with Kanu scoring twice, including the winning "golden goal"), and then Argentina to take the gold medal. Kanu was voted African Footballer of the Year in 1996 and again in 1999. He played in the 1998 and 2002 World Cups.

Right: Kanu celebrates an Arsenal goal.

Roy Keane
(Ireland, b. 1971)

Clubs: *Nottingham Forest (1990–93), Manchester United (1993–)*
Caps: *58 (9 goals)*

A strong, aggressive, ball-winning midfielder, with a fiery temper and a commanding on-pitch manner, Keane is also a skilful passer and he has a knack for scoring important goals. He left his native Cork for Brian Clough's Nottingham Forest in 1990, and he moved to Manchester United three years later, becoming captain in 1997. A crucial member of Ferguson's team, he has amassed five league titles and three FA Cups, as well as a European Cup winner's medal, although he missed the 1999 final against Bayern Munich due to suspension, and was injured for the entire 1997–98 season. His own goal in the 2000 European Cup quarter-final helped Real Madrid qualify for the semi-finals. As captain of the Republic of Ireland squad for the 2002 World Cup finals, he was sent home before the start after disagreements with management.

Left: Roy Keane, Manchester United's hard-tackling midfielder.

Above: Kevin Keegan: "Mighty Mouse" of Liverpool, Hamburg and England.

Mario Kempes
(Argentina, b. 1954)

Clubs: *Instituto de Cordoba (1967–70), Rosario Central (1970–76), Valéncia (1976–81), River Plate (1981–82)*
Caps: *43 (20 goals)*

A long-haired, muscular centre-forward, Kempes was transferred from Rosario to Valéncia in 1976, having played for Argentina in the 1974 World Cup finals. The high point of his career came in the 1978 World Cup where, playing in front of his home crowd, he was voted Player of the Tournament. He scored six goals, including two in the final against Holland. The first was a touch-in from a Luque pass and the second, in extra time, was a superb solo goal past three Dutch defenders. He then supplied Bertoni with the pass that set up the third goal in Argentina's 3–1 triumph. He was voted South American Player of the Year in 1978. In 1980 he won a Cup Winners Cup medal with Valéncia, but in 1981 he returned to Argentina. He played in the 1982 World Cup, but he and Argentina were ineffectual in the tournament.

Kevin Keegan
(England, b. 1951)

Clubs: *Scunthorpe United (1968–71), Liverpool (1971–77), Hamburg (1977–80), Southampton (1980–82), Newcastle United (1982–84)*
Caps: *63 (21 goals)*

A small, dynamic creator and finisher, Keegan starred for Liverpool and England in the 1970s. Bought by Bill Shankly in 1971, he soon established himself in attack alongside John Toshack. Liverpool won the league twice and the 1976 UEFA Cup, with Keegan scoring in both legs of the final, and he was voted Footballer of the Year. He produced a fine performance the following year in the European Cup Final against Borussia Mönchengladbach (Liverpool won 3–1), and he moved to Hamburg in the summer of 1977. While at Hamburg he was twice voted European Footballer of the Year, and he played in Hamburg's losing team in the 1980 European Cup Final against Nottingham Forest. Keegan returned to English football in 1980 to join Southampton, and then Newcastle in 1982, where his goals helped United gain promotion to the First Division. Keegan gained his first international cap in 1972 and he played for his country for ten years, eventually being dropped in 1982. After his playing career ended, Keegan became manager of Newcastle United, Fulham and in 1999 England. He resigned in 2000 after England lost a World Cup qualifying match against Germany and guided Manchester City to the Premiership in 2002.

Above: Mario Kempes celebrates as Argentina wins its first World Cup in 1978.

Jürgen Klinsmann (Germany, b. 1964)

Clubs: *Stuttgart Kickers (1980–84), VfB Stuttgart (1984–89), Inter Milan (1989–92), Monaco (1992–94), Tottenham Hotspur (1994–95), Bayern Munich (1995–97), Sampdoria (1997), Tottenham Hotspur (1997–98)*
Caps: *108 (47 goals)*

Below: Jürgen Klinsman during his first spell with Spurs in 1994–95.

Klinsmann is Germany's second-highest goal scorer (the highest is Gerd Müller). A top-class striker, with sharp anticipation and acceleration, Klinsmann moved from VfB Stuttgart in 1989 to join Inter Milan, where he won a UEFA Cup winner's medal in 1991. His three goals in the tournament helped Germany to win the 1990 World Cup Final, and he moved to Monaco that summer. He scored five goals for Germany in the 1994 World Cup finals, but the team was eliminated by Bulgaria in the quarter-finals. That autumn,

Klinsmann made a surprising £2-million move to Tottenham Hotspur. By the end of the season he had scored 20 goals for the north London side, and been voted Footballer of the Year. He then moved to Bayern Munich, and he scored a record 15 goals in their progress through the 1995–96 UEFA Cup, which Bayern won 5–1 on aggregate against Bordeaux in the final. Klinsmann captained his country to victory in Euro '96, and he led Germany to the 1998 World Cup finals, but they were eliminated 3–0 by Croatia in their quarter-final.

Patrick Kluivert
(Holland, b. 1976)

Clubs: *Ajax (1994–97), AC Milan (1997–98), Barcelona (1998–)*
Caps: *67 (36 goals)*

A fast and powerful young striker, Kluivert is yet another successful product of the Ajax youth system. Playing in attack with Marc Overmars and Jari Litmanen, Kluivert's goals helped Ajax win the Dutch league title in 1995 and 1996. He also scored the winning goal, with five minutes to go, in the 1995 European Cup Final against AC Milan, and came on as a substitute in the final the following year against Juventus. He joined AC Milan in 1997 but had a frustrating time due to injury, and he was bought by mentor and former Ajax manager Louis Van Gaal for Barcelona the following year. He forced Brazil's Sonny Anderson out of the first team, and his understanding with Luis Figo and Rivaldo took Barcelona to the semi-final of the 2000 European Cup. He played for Holland in Euro '96, and his two goals against Yugoslavia and Argentina helped Holland secure fourth place in the 1998 World Cup finals. Kluivert was joint top scorer at Euro 2000, and his five goals eased Holland's passage to the semi-finals.

Right: Kluivert with the European Cup.

Sandor Kocsis
(Hungary, 1928–1979)

Clubs: *Ferencvaros (1944–49), Honved (1949–55), Young Boys Berne (1955–56), Barcelona (1956–63)*
Caps: *68 (75 goals)*

Another of the "Magnificent Magyars", inside-right Kocsis played alongside Ferenc Puskas in the Honved and

Left: Sandor Kocsis (centre), lining up with the Hungarian team to play England at Wembley in 1953.

Hungary teams of the early 1950s. He was top scorer in the 1954 World Cup finals with 11 goals, including two in the semi-final against Uruguay. He joined Barcelona after the 1956 Hungarian revolution. He helped the Spanish club to a Fairs Cup victory over Birmingham in 1960, and scored in their 3–2 defeat by Benfica in the 1961 European Cup Final. Kocsis scored all three of Barcelona's goals in the 7–3 aggregate defeat by Valéncia in the 1962 Fairs Cup Final. He won three Hungarian league titles with Honved, and one Spanish league title with Barcelona. Kocsis died in 1979.

Ronald Koeman
(Holland, b. 1963)

Clubs: *Groningen (1980–83), Ajax (1983–86), PSV Eindhoven (1986–89), Barcelona (1989–95), Feyenoord (1995–98)*
Caps: *77 (14 goals)*

The blond-haired Koeman was a stocky, attacking sweeper with a thunderbolt shot, particularly from free kicks. He moved from Ajax to PSV Eindhoven in 1986, where he scored 21 goals in his first season. In 1988 he won a European Cup winner's medal when PSV beat Benfica, and he signed for Barcelona the following year. Koeman scored in Barcelona's 2–1 European Cup Winners Cup defeat by Manchester United in 1991, and he scored again with an extra-time rocket of a strike to win the European Cup for his club, in 1992, against Sampdoria. He was a member of Holland's victorious team in the 1988 European Championships, and he played in the 1990 and 1994 World Cup finals. Koeman left Barcelona in 1995 to return to club football in Holland. He retired in 1998.

Right: The muscular, blond figure of Holland's Ronald Koeman.

Raymond Kopa
(Kopaszewski)
(France, b. 1931)

Clubs: *Angiers (1949–51), Reims (1951–56), Real Madrid (1956–59), Reims (1959–67)*
Caps: *45 (18 goals)*

The son of an immigrant Polish miner, Kopa was a centre-forward of skill, poise and balance. He began his career on the right wing at Angiers, in Algeria, and joined the French club Reims in 1951, moving into the centre position. After playing against Real Madrid in the 1956 European Cup Final, Kopa joined the Spanish club but he returned to his former position on the wing to accommodate the great Alfredo Di Stefano. He played in Real's next three European Cup victories and returned to Reims in 1959, where he won the French league in his first season back with the club. Kopa gained 45 caps for France, playing alongside Just Fontaine for the 1954 and 1958 World Cup finals; the pair enjoyed a highly successful partnership at the front. Kopa scored three goals in the World Cup of 1958, where France reached third place, with a total of 18 goals in his international career.

Left: Raymond Kopa in action for Real Madrid.

Ruud Krol
(Holland, b. 1949)

Clubs: *Ajax (1964–80), Vancouver Whitecaps (1980), Napoli (1980–82)*
Caps: *83 (2 goals)*

A big, attacking centre-back, Krol is the most-capped player in Dutch football history. Playing for Ajax, along with Johann Cruyff, Günter Neeskens and Johnny Rep, he was a vital cog in Rinus Michels' "total football" system. He collected two European Cup winner's medals in 1972 and 1973, beating Inter Milan and Juventus respectively in the finals. He made his international debut in 1969 and played in two World Cup Finals – against West Germany in 1974 and, as sweeper, against Argentina in 1978 – losing them both. He was one of the last of the great team to leave Ajax, and by the time he moved to his last club Napoli in 1980, he had won six Dutch league titles.

Right: Ruud Krol (right) playing for Holland against West Germany in the 1974 World Cup Final.

Ladislav Kubala
(Hungary, 1927–2002)

Clubs: *Ferencvaros, Bratislava, Vasas, Barcelona, Espanyol, FC Zürich*
Caps: *3 (Hungary), 7 (4 goals) (Czechoslovkia), 19 (10 goals) (Spain)*

Hungarian inside-forward Kubala escaped from Eastern Europe in the immediate post-war climate of the late 1940s. He signed for Barcelona, and was later joined there by his

Left: Hungarian exile Kubala gained most of his club honours in Spain.

compatriots and fellow exiles, Zoltan Czibor and Sandor Kocsis. Between them, the Hungarians created a much-feared forward line, which helped Barcelona to the European Cup Final and to two Fairs Cup victories. Kubala also achieved six Spanish league and six Spanish Cup titles with Barcelona for whom he scored 243 goals in 329 games, before moving to Espanyol and then FC Zürich. He played for Zürich in 1967, at the age of 39, in a European Cup tie against Celtic. He finished his playing career in Canada. Kubala was capped by three different countries, and he was also selected for the FIFA "Rest of the World" side that played against England in 1963.

Grzegorz Lato
(Poland, b. 1950)

Clubs: *Stal Mielec, Lokeren, Atlante*
Caps: *104 (45 goals)*

Poland's most-capped player, the predatory Grzegorz Lato, began his career as a right-winger with Polish club Stal Mielec, and he moved into midfield later in his career. He won two Polish league titles with Stal, before signing for the Belgian club Lokeren.

He finished his club football with Atlante in Mexico. Playing alongside Deyna and Gadocha in the strong Polish international side, Lato was top goal scorer, with seven goals, in the 1974 World Cup finals – the last goal was scored against Brazil with only 15 minutes to go, securing Poland's third place. Lato also played in the 1978 finals, but this time the team had less success.

Right: Grzegorz Lato, leading scorer in the 1974 World Cup finals.

Michael Laudrup
(Denmark, b. 1964)

Clubs: *Brondby (1978–83), Lazio (1983–85), Juventus (1985–89), Barcelona (1989–94), Real Madrid (1994–96), Vissel Kobe (1996–97), Ajax (1997–98)*
Caps: *104 (37 goals)*

Laudrup was an elegant midfielder and Denmark's most-capped outfield player with 104 international appearances to his name. He began his playing career with Brondby, before moving to Italy,

Left: Michael Laudrup playing for Denmark. Laudrup made three World Cup appearances for his country.

first to Lazio, and then to Juventus in 1985. In 1989 he moved to Barcelona, where his perceptive passing and attacking skills helped them to their first European Cup title in 1992, and to four consecutive Spanish league titles. He then transferred to Real Madrid, where he inspired the Spanish club to win the league. In 1996 Laudrup moved to the Japanese side Vissel Kobe. He made his international debut at the age of 18, and has played in the 1986, 1990 and 1998 World Cup finals. However, he missed out on Denmark's surprise 1992 European Championship victory after a dispute with coach Richard Moller Nielsen left him on the bench. Laudrup has now retired from international football.

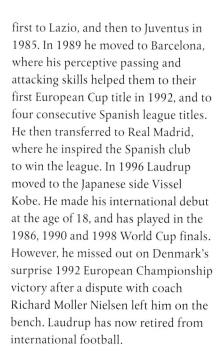

Denis Law
(Scotland, b. 1940)

Clubs: *Huddersfield Town (1957–60), Manchester City (1960–61), Torino (1961), Manchester United (1961–73), Manchester City (1973–74)*
Caps: *55 (30 goals)*

"The Lawman" was a slim, fair-haired striker of medium build, but he was lethal in the penalty box and in the air for Manchester United and Scotland. He joined Manchester City from Huddersfield for a record £55,000 fee in 1960, spent a few unhappy months with Torino, and joined Manchester United for £116,000 in 1961. Over the next few years his goal scoring, and his partnership with Best and Charlton brought two league titles to Matt Busby's side, in 1965 and 1967, and he was prolific in European games, scoring four hat tricks. However, he missed the club's 1968 European Cup Final victory due to injury. Law was first capped at the age of 18 and, though he only played in one World Cup finals, in 1974, he scored 30 goals for his country. He was selected for the FIFA "Rest of the World" side that played against England, in 1963, and he scored in the match. He moved to Manchester City in 1973, and his goal helped to send United into the Second Division in 1974, the year he retired.

Above: Denis Law adds to his goal tally for Manchester United in the 1971–2 season.

Tommy Lawton
(England, 1919–1996)

Clubs: *Burnley (1936–37), Everton (1937–45), Chelsea (1945–47), Notts County (1947–52), Brentford (1952–53), Arsenal (1953–56)*
Caps: *23 (22 goals)*

A direct, exciting centre-forward, Lawton joined Burnley in 1936 and became, at the age of 17, the youngest player to score a hat trick in the

Left: Lawton, in his Arsenal strip, towards the end of his playing career.

Football League. He moved to Everton the following year, as a replacement for "Dixie" Dean, and was top scorer in both 1938 and 1939, the year Everton won the English league title. In 1939 he made his international debut against Wales and scored. He joined Chelsea after World War Two and then moved to Notts County in 1947, for a record £20,000 fee. His 31 goals secured promotion for County in 1950, and Lawton moved on again to become player-manager of Brentford. He spent a couple of seasons with Arsenal before becoming manager of Kettering Town. Tommy Lawton died in 1996.

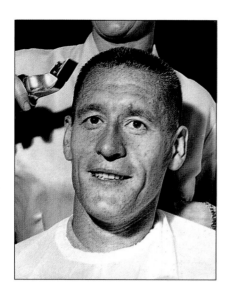

Nils Liedholm
(Sweden, 1922–2000)

Clubs: *Norköpping (1948–49), AC Milan (1949–61)*
Caps: *23 (11 goals)*

Liedholm was one-third of the "Gre-no-li" Swedish attack that brought AC Milan the *Serie A* title in 1951, for the first time in 44 years. He was an inside-forward with great skill and an exceptional shot, who had

Left: The skilful Swede Nils Liedholm.

joined Milan shortly after picking up an Olympic gold medal, when Sweden beat Yugoslavia in the final of the 1948 games. Liedholm played in the 1958 European Cup Final against Real Madrid, making the first goal for Schiaffino, but Milan lost 3–2 in extra time. He captained Sweden to the 1958 World Cup Final and scored the opening goal in the first four minutes, only to lose 5–2 to an exuberant Brazil. After retirement, Liedholm became Milan's coach, and also managed Fiorentina and Roma, whom he took to the 1984 European Cup Final.

Gary Lineker
(England, b. 1960)

Clubs: *Leicester City (1978–85), Everton (1985–86), Barcelona (1986–89), Tottenham Hotspur (1989–92), Grampus Eight (1992–94)*
Caps: *80 (48 goals)*

Lineker is England's second-highest goal scorer with 48 goals, one behind Bobby Charlton. A deadly finisher in the penalty area, he moved from Leicester to Everton in 1985; that season he scored 30 goals for the club and was voted Player of the Year. In 1986, he scored six goals for England in the World Cup finals, including a hat trick against Poland, and he finished as the tournament's top scorer. The same year Lineker moved to Barcelona, and his goals helped the club win the European Cup Winners Cup in 1989. He moved to Spurs in 1989 and the scoring continued, with Lineker netting a total of 28 league goals in 1991–92. In the 1990 World Cup, Lineker's two late goals saved England from embarrassment against Cameroon in the quarter-finals, although his late equalizer against Germany could not prevent England's elimination from the tournament on penalties in the semi-final. He moved to Japan to play with Grampus Eight, and, in the mid-1990s, came back to England to start a broadcasting career.

Above: Gary Lineker, Spurs' and England's high-scoring centre-forward.

Sepp Maier
(Germany, b. 1944)

Clubs: *Bayern Munich
(1960–1979)*
Caps: *95*

Maier was West Germany's best and most consistent keeper in the 1970s. He spent the bulk of his career with Bayern Munich, making a total of 422 consecutive appearances for the

Left: Sepp Maier grabs the ball for West Germany against Italy.

Bavarians. He was in goal for Bayern's 1967 extra-time 1–0 European Cup Winners Cup victory over Rangers and for their three European Cup victories. In particular, Maier's athletic and acrobatic performances in the 1975 final against Leeds United, and the 1976 final against Saint Etienne, helped Bayern lift the trophies. He also won four *Bundesliga* titles with Bayern. At international level Maier had an exceptional match in West Germany's 2–1 win over Holland in the 1974 World Cup Final. A road accident in 1979 ended his footballing career.

Paolo Maldini
(Italy, b. 1968)

Clubs: *AC Milan (1985–)*
Caps: *126 (7 goals)*

Son of ex-AC Milan captain and ex-Italian manager Cesare Maldini, Paolo has carved out his own name in football as probaby the best defender in the world. His cool and efficient tackling and sudden surges into attack mark him out as a special player, and the left-back position at Milan has been his since 1985. He has won six *Serie A* titles and four European Cup winner's medals, and has made over 400 appearances for the club. Maldini made his international debut in 1988, against Yugoslavia, at the age of 19. He played in the 1990, 1994, 1998 and 2002 World Cup finals, the last two as captain. He was also captain of Italy in Euro '96 and 2000. He was voted World Player of the Year in 1994, and is the most-capped player in Italian footballing history. Maldini's heroic efforts in the Euro 2000 Final against France were not enough for Italy to lift the trophy. Sadly, his final international coincided with Italy's exit from the 2002 World Cup, defeated by South Korea. He won his fourth European Cup winner's medal in 2003, when AC Milan beat rivals Juventus in the Champions League Final.

Right: Paolo Maldini, captain of Italy.

Diego Maradona
(Argentina, b. 1960)

Clubs: *Argentinos Juniors (1976–80), Boca Juniors (1980–82), Barcelona (1982–84), Napoli (1984–92), Seville (1992–93), Newell's Old Boys (1993–95), Boca Juniors (1995–97)*
Caps: *91 (34 goals)*

Maradona was at one time the best footballer in the world, and some say the best ever. Whatever his ranking, there is no doubt that Maradona was immensely skilled, with exquisite touch and control, a lethal left foot and electric pace. His talents saw him leave Argentina for a world-record fee of £4.2 million, in 1982, to join Barcelona, where he suffered a bruising couple of seasons. He moved to Napoli in 1984 for a new world-record fee of £5 million, and by the end of the decade he had brought the club the Italian "double", in 1987, and the UEFA Cup, in 1989. He appeared for Argentina in the 1982 World Cup finals, being sent off against Brazil, and in 1986 he captained his country to World Cup triumph. He scored brilliant solo goals against England

Above: Diego Maradona, voted the greatest player of the 20th century.

and Belgium, and was named Player of the Tournament. He was again captain in the 1990 competition but Argentina lost a poor final to West Germany. A 15-months drugs ban followed, and he returned to Argentina in 1993. He played in the 1994 World Cup finals, but was sent home after failing another drugs test. Maradona retired in 1997, an exceptional talent destroyed by drugs and self-indulgence. In a FIFA poll, he was voted, with Pelé, joint Player of the Twentieth Century.

Josef Masopust (Czechoslovakia, 1931–2000)

Clubs: *Teplice (1948–51), Dukla Prague (1951–68), Molenbeek (1968–70)*
Caps: *63 (10 goals)*

A clever, elegant left-half, Masopust was the creative force behind the Czech and Dukla Prague teams of the 1950s

and 1960s. He led his country to third place in the 1960 European Championships, and he scored the first goal in the 1962 World Cup Final – only for Brazil to score three and retain the trophy. That year Masopust was voted European Footballer of the Year. He won eight Czech league titles with Dukla Prague between 1953 and 1966.

Right: Masopust, playmaker of Czechoslovakia in the early 1960s.

Lothar Matthäus (Germany, b. 1961)

Clubs: *Borussia Mönchengladbach (1978–84), Bayern Munich (1984–88), Inter Milan (1988–92), Bayern Munich (1992–2000), New Jersey Metrostars (2000–)*
Caps: *144 (22 goals)*

Matthäus is the most-capped player in German football history, and has gained more caps than any other player in the world. A determined, ball-winning midfielder, his presence has pervaded German football over the last two decades. His spiky attitude and outspoken manner have alienated team-mates and fans over the years, but no one can question his talent. He joined Bayern Munich in 1984 and won three consecutive *Bundesliga* titles from 1985–87. He moved to Inter Milan in 1988, and won a *Serie A* title in his first season and a UEFA Cup winner's medal in 1991. He played in the 1986 World Cup Final, marking Maradona, and in 1990, as captain, he led Germany to victory over Argentina and was voted World Footballer of the Year. He played again in 1994 and, to the surprise of many, was selected for the 1998 tournament. He moved back to Bayern in 1992 and helped the club to two further *Bundesliga* titles in 1994 and 1997, and to a UEFA Cup victory in 1996. Bayern lost to Manchester United in the dying seconds of the 1999 European Cup Final, and Matthäus decided it was time to go. He joined the New Jersey-based Metrostars in 2000.

Above: Matthäus, the irascible captain of Germany at Italia '90.

Stanley Matthews
(England, 1915–2000)

Clubs: *Stoke City (1930–47),
Blackpool (1947–61), Stoke City
(1961–65)*
Caps: *54 (11 goals)*

Matthews, the "Wizard of Dribble",
was a dazzling winger with sublime
feinting and dribbling skills. His ability
to take on and beat defenders was
breathtaking, he could cross the ball
with deadly accuracy, and he was a
regular on the England right wing for
over 20 years. A hero at Stoke City for
17 years, he left the club in 1947 to
join Blackpool. In the 1953 FA Cup
Final he inspired Blackpool, 3–1
down to Bolton in the second half,
to a 4–3 victory, and the game is still
remembered as "the Matthews Final".
He was first capped in 1934 and played
in the 1950 and 1954 World Cup
finals, and he won the first European
Footballer of the Year award in 1956;
that year he also received a CBE. He
rejoined Stoke at the age of 46, and
continued playing until the age of 50,
the oldest player ever to appear in the
First Division. To mark his retirement
he was awarded a knighthood. He died,
to universal mourning, in 2000.

*Left: Stanley Matthews, about
to launch another cross to his
waiting forwards.*

Alessandro "Sandro"
Mazzola (Italy, b. 1942)

Clubs: *Inter Milan (1960–74)*
Caps: *70 (22 goals)*

Son of Valentino, the Torino captain
who was killed in the 1949 Superga
air crash, Mazzola was a tall, cultured
inside-forward who spent his entire
career with Inter Milan. He won his
first *Serie A* league medal in 1963, and
three more in 1965, 1966 and 1971,
and played in three European Cup
finals that decade. In the 1964 final,
his two goals helped to finish off
Real Madrid in Inter's 3–1 victory, and
the following year Inter beat Benfica
1–0 in the final. In the 1967 European
Cup Final Mazzola scored first against
Celtic, but Jock Stein's men ran out the
eventual 2–1 winners. He also played
in the 1972 final, but this time it was
Ajax that beat the Italian side 2–0.
Mazzola was first capped in 1963, in
a game against Brazil, scoring on his
debut. He played in the Italian side
that won both the 1968 European
Championship and finished runners-
up in the 1970 World Cup Final.

Right: Mazzola at the 1970 World Cup.

Billy McNeill
(Scotland, b. 1940)

Clubs: *Celtic (1957–75)*
Caps: *29 (3 goals)*

McNeill, known as "Caesar" for his imperious leadership and coolness under pressure, was centre-half and captain of Jock Stein's great Celtic side in the 1960s and early 1970s. A one-club man, McNeill steered Celtic to the European Cup Final in 1967, scoring a rare goal and the winner against Vojvodina Novi Sad in the quarter-final at Parkhead, and became the first British footballer ever to lift the trophy after Celtic's 2–1 victory over Inter Milan in the final in Lisbon. He also collected nine league winner's medals and seven Scottish Cups in his 832 appearances for Celtic. He made his first appearance for Scotland in 1961, when the Scots were hammered 9–3 by England at Wembley, and gained 29 caps. When his playing career ended McNeill managed Celtic, Aston Villa and Manchester City. He was awarded an MBE in 1974.

Above: Celtic's captain and centre-half Billy McNeill.

Above: Meazza collects the Jules Rimet trophy as Italy win the World Cup of 1938.

Giuseppe Meazza
(Italy, 1910–1979)

Clubs: *Ambrosiana (Inter Milan) (1927–40), AC Milan (1940–42), Juventus (1942–43), Atalanta (1945–46), Inter Milan (1946–48)*
Caps: *53 (33 goals)*

Italy's second-highest goal scorer after Gigi Rivi, Meazza is only one of two players to have appeared in Italy's two World Cup Final triumphs in 1934 and 1938, the other being Giovanni Ferrari. Meazza was captain of the 1938 team, and he scored the winning goal, from the penalty spot, in the semi-final against Brazil. He played his first game for Inter Milan in 1927, and collected two *Serie A* winner's medals before moving to AC Milan in 1938. He ended his career at Inter, and when he died in 1979 the San Siro stadium was named after him as a tribute from the city of Milan.

Above: Roger Milla at Italia '90.

Roger Milla
(Cameroon, b. 1952)

Clubs: *Tannerre Yaounde (1967–76), Valenciennes (1976–78), Monaco (1978–80), Bastia (1981–87), Saint Etienne (1987–2000)*
Caps: *81 (42 goals)*

Milla was the unlikely star of the 1990 World Cup finals. In the opening game, his unfancied Cameroon team beat defending champions Argentina 1–0, and they reached the quarter-finals, where only an extra-time penalty from Gary Lineker denied them further progress. Milla ended the tournament with four goals, and he delighted the crowds and the massive television audience with his flamboyant celebrations around the corner flag. He played again for Cameroon in the 1994 World Cup tournament in the United States – but this time with rather less success – and at the age of 42 he became the oldest player ever to play in a World Cup finals. He joined Valenciennes from Cameroon in 1976, and he spent his career with a variety of French clubs. Milla has been twice voted African Player of the Year, in 1976 and 1990. He retired in 2000.

Bobby Moore
(England, 1941–1993)

Clubs: *West Ham United (1958–74), Fulham (1974–76), Seattle Sounders (1976), San Antonio Thunder (1978)*
Caps: *108 (3 goals)*

A graceful, intelligent player, Moore was the defensive pivot of England and West Ham in the 1960s. His ability to read a game, his sharpness in the tackle and his passing skills brought him a total of 108 caps, an achievement that has been eclipsed only by Peter Shilton. Moore played his first game for West Ham at the age of 17, and he captained the Hammers to the FA Cup in 1964 and the Cup Winners Cup in 1965, beating 1860 Munich 2–0. Moore was first capped in 1962, and was made captain the following year. He was captain when England won the World Cup in 1966, and it was his pass that set up Hurst's third goal. He was named Player of the Tournament, and was awarded an OBE in 1967. In the 1970 World Cup finals he produced a magnificent performance against Pelé's Brazil in the group stage, but England were eliminated by West Germany in the quarter-final. He joined Fulham in 1974, later leaving to play in the United States. Moore retired in 1978 to pursue an unsuccessful management career. He died from cancer in 1993, aged 51.

Above: Bobby Moore, captain of West Ham and England.

Stan Mortensen
(England, 1921–1991)

Clubs: *Blackpool (1939–55),*
Hull City (1955–57),
Southport (1957–60)
Caps: *25 (23 goals)*

Mortenson was a speedy, goal-scoring centre-forward, with one of the strongest shots in English football. Nicknamed the "Electric Eel" for his ability to slither past defenders, he spent most of his career with Blackpool, playing alongside Stanley Matthews. In 1948 he scored in every round of the FA Cup, including the final where Blackpool lost to Manchester United, and he scored a hat trick in the 1953 final, bringing Blackpool their only major honour. He made his international debut in 1947, and scored four goals in England's 10–0 crushing win over Portugal. He scored another three goals against Sweden later that year. He played in England's disastrous 1950 World Cup finals, and he won his last cap in England's 6–3 defeat by Puskas' Hungary in 1953. He was manager of Blackpool for a brief period in the late 1960s. Stan Mortensen died in 1991.

Above: Mortensen heads goalwards for Blackpool against Wolves in 1953.

Gerd Müller
(Germany, b. 1945)

Clubs: *TSV Nordlingen (1962–64),*
Bayern Munich (1964–79), Fort
Lauderdale Strikers (1979–81)
Caps: *62 (68 goals)*

A stocky figure, Müller did not give the appearance of being a top footballer. However, he won three European Cup and a World Cup winner's medals, and he is the highest scorer in German international history. Müller was a natural striker, with fast reflexes and keen awareness, and he rarely squandered an opportunity inside the penalty box. Known as *"Der Bomber"*, he spent nearly 16 years at Bayern Munich, where he scored 365 goals in 427 league matches, and won the European Cup in 1974, 1975 and 1976, as well as the *Bundesliga* four times. The international heir to the great Uwe Seeler, Müller scored ten goals in the 1970 World Cup finals and two in the 1972 European Championship Final against the Soviet Union. He claimed another four in 1974, when West Germany won the tournament, thanks to his goal in the final. Müller was named European Footballer of the Year in 1970.

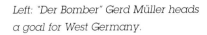

Left: "Der Bomber" Gerd Müller heads a goal for West Germany.

Johan Neeskens
(Holland, b. 1951)

Clubs: *Ajax (1967–74), Barcelona (1974–80), New York Cosmos (1980–85), Groningen (1985–86)*
Caps: *49 (17 goals)*

An intelligent midfielder with a strong right-foot shot and a tough tackle, the 19-year-old Neeskens broke into the Ajax first team in 1970. He played in all three of Ajax's consecutive European Cup victories from 1971–73, supplying the ball to Cruyff and Swart in attack.

Left: Ajax and Holland midfielder Johan Neeskens connects with the ball.

Neeskens scored Holland's second-minute goal from the penalty spot in the 1974 World Cup Final, when Cruyff was fouled in the box, and he was the second top scorer of the tournament that year, with five goals. Neeskens played again in the final four years later, in 1978, with Holland losing 3–1 to Argentina. At club level he followed his Ajax and Holland team-mate Cruyff to Barcelona, in 1974, and helped the club win the European Cup Winner's Cup in 1979. He played his football in the United States the following season, returning to Holland five years later to take his place with Groningen, where he played out his career until his retirement.

Günter Netzer
(Germany, b. 1944)

Clubs: *Borussia Mönchengladbach (1961–73), Real Madrid (1973–76), Grasshoppers Zurich (1976–78)*
Caps: *37 (6 goals)*

Netzer's extravagant skills were the inspiration behind West Germany's 1972 European Championship triumph, with the long-haired midfield supremo linking play between Franz Beckenbauer and Gerd Müller. Netzer began his career with Borussia Mönchengladbach and led the club to two *Bundesliga* titles in 1970 and 1971. He left to join Real Madrid in 1973, and was dropped by German manager Helmut Schön for the 1974 World Cup Final. He won two Spanish league titles in 1975 and 1976. He spent two seasons in Switzerland with Grasshoppers before retiring as a player in 1978. Netzer's first assignment as a manager was with Hamburg, and he helped the club to their first *Bundesliga* title in 19 years, as well as to the final of the 1979–80 European Cup.

Right: Netzer (right) in the 1972 European Championship Final against the USSR.

Gunnar Nordahl
(Sweden, 1921–1995)

Clubs: *Degerfors (1940–44),
IFK Nörrkoping (1944–49),
AC Milan (1949–56),
Roma (1956–59)*
Caps: *33 (43 goals)*

*Left: The strong, dependable Gunnar
Nordhal. Along with Gunnar Gren
and Nils Liedholm, he was one of the
Swedish trio in attack for AC Milan
during the early 1950s.*

A strong, consistent goal scorer,
Nordahl helped Nörrkoping to four
Swedish league titles before joining
AC Milan to become part of the
so-called "Gre-no-li" trio. That season
he scored ten goals in *Serie A*. He was
top scorer in 1949–50 with 35 goals,
and top scorer again with 34 goals in
1950–51, when Milan took their first
title in 44 years; he repeated the feat
three years in succession from
1953–55. He won an Olympic gold
medal with Sweden in 1948; it was
to be his last cap for his country.

Wolfgang Overath
(Germany, b. 1943)

Clubs: *Cologne (1962–77)*
Caps: *81 (17 goals)*

Inside-left Overath joined his home
club Cologne in 1962, and stayed there
until his retirement in 1977. He was
capped in 1963, and in 1964 Cologne
won the newly instituted *Bundesliga*
title. He played in the German side
which lost 4–2 to England in the 1966
World Cup Final, and he played again
in the 1970 finals, scoring the goal
against Uruguay that gave West
Germany third-place spot. Günter
Netzer was preferred to Overath in the
1972 European Championships, but
Overath ousted Netzer for the 1974
World Cup finals, where he won a
winner's medal when Germany beat
Holland 2–1 in the final. He retired
from international football after that
tournament.

*Right: One-club man Wolfgang
Overath playing for West Germany
in the 1974 World Cup, which they
hosted. Overath had played in two
previous World Cup finals, in 1966
and 1970, but it was in 1974 that his
country took the World Champions title.*

Ariel Ortega
(Argentina, b. 1974)

Clubs: *River Plate (1991–97), Valéncia (1997–98), Sampdoria (1998–99), Parma (1999–2000), River Plate (2000–2002), Fenerbahce (2002–2003)*
Caps: *84 (17 goals)*

Small, tricky midfielder Ortega made his debut for Argentina's River Plate in 1991 and helped the club win the *Copa Libertadores* and the Argentinian

Left: Argentinian midfielder Ariel Ortega.

league in 1994 before moving to Valéncia in 1997. His first international was in 1993, and he was called up to replace a disgraced Maradona in the middle of the 1994 World Cup finals. He won a silver medal in the Atlanta Olympics in 1996, and scored five goals in the qualifiers for the 1998 World Cup finals. In that tournament, Argentina were knocked out in the quarter-final by Holland, and Ortega was sent off for head-butting the Dutch keeper. He appeared in the 2002 World Cup finals. He moved to River Plate on loan in 2000, and in 2002 he joined Fenerbahce but was sacked in 2003.

Michael Owen
(England, b. 1979)

Clubs: *Liverpool (1996–)*
Caps: *50 (22 goals)*

A small, explosively fast striker, Owen is one of the brightest talents to have emerged from the English game in recent years. A trainee at Liverpool, Owen made his debut in 1997 against Wimbledon and scored in his first game. By the end of the 1997–98 season he had scored 18 league goals, and he bettered it with 23 the following season. At 18 years and two months, Owen was the youngest player to have played for England in the 20th century, and he has already gained 26 caps. He played in the 1998 World Cup finals and scored a memorable goal against Argentina, when he danced through the defence and lashed an unstoppable shot into the net. Owen was injured for much of the 1999–2000 season, but he was back in the team in 2000–1, when he scored the two goals against Arsenal that won the FA Cup for Liverpool. He scored a hat-trick in England's 5–1 defeat of Germany in Munich on the way to the 2002 World Cup finals, where he scored against Brazil. He was European Footballer of the Year in 2001.

Right: Striker Michael Owen has made himself an England regular.

Jean-Pierre Papin
(France, b. 1963)

Clubs: *Valenciennes (1984–85), Bruges (1985–86), Marseille (1986–92), AC Milan (1992–94), Bayern Munich (1994–96), Bordeaux (1996–98)*
Caps: *54 (30 goals)*

A deadly striker, Papin was the French league's top goal scorer four times in the late 1980s, and one of the leading strikers of the modern game. Papin began his career with French club Valenciennes, before moving to the Belgian side Bruges in 1985. He returned to France a year later, and quickly became the captain and inspiration for the Bernard Tapie-funded Marseille. His goals helped Marseille to win the league title for four years in succession. He played in the 1991 European Cup Final in Bari, when Marseille were beaten on penalties by Red Star Belgrade. That year he was voted European Footballer of the Year. He also played in the 1993 final, this time for AC Milan, and was again on the losing side (ironically, the 1–0 winners were Marseille). Papin was transferred to Bayern Munich in 1994, and he received his last French cap in 1995. His two years at Bordeaux – the last years of his playing career – were marred by injury.

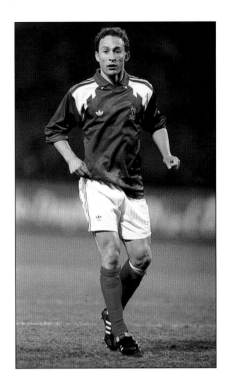

Right: Jean-Pierre Papin, a much-travelled striker, in his national strip.

Daniel Passarella
(Argentina, b. 1953)

Clubs: *Sarmiento (1971–73), River Plate (1974–82), Fiorentina (1982–86), Inter Milan (1986–88), River Plate (1988–89)*
Caps: *70 (22 goals)*

A commanding centre-half with an eye for goal, Passarella was captain of the River Plate team that won four Argentinian league titles in the 1970s. In 1978 his defensive play powered Argentina to victory in the World Cup Final, with Passarella collecting the trophy as captain. His playing career in Europe included first Fiorentina and then Inter Milan, but he returned to Argentina as the manager of River Plate. He was manager of Argentina for the 1998 World Cup finals, and his side reached the quarter-finals, where they were eliminated by Holland and a last-minute wondergoal from Dennis Bergkamp. Passarella managed the Uruguay national team for a short spell from 1999.

Right: Passarella (right) rises to prevent an Italian attack.

Pelé, Edison Arantes do Nascimento (Brazil, b. 1940)

Clubs: *Santos (1956–74), New York Cosmos (1975–77)*
Caps: *91 (77 goals)*

Pelé is generally regarded as the finest player ever to have graced the game. His passing and dribbling skills were breathtaking, his finishing ability was lethally accurate, and he had abundant pace and strength. He was, in short, the perfect footballer. He played all his club football with Brazilian side Santos and, latterly New York Cosmos, but he will be most remembered for his World Cup performances. In 1958, the 17-year-old Pelé scored twice in the 5–2 win over Sweden in the final, to add to the hat trick he collected against France in the semi-final. He was injured for the 1962 tournament and, as a marked man in the finals of 1966, he was brutally kicked off the pitch by Portugal. However, in the Mexico finals of 1970, Pelé was the undoubted star of the show. In the final he scored a remarkable header, and made two more goals to help Brazil beat Italy 4–1 and become the World Champions. When Pelé left Santos, his number ten shirt was permanently removed from the line-up as a tribute to him. He retired in 1977 and became Minister for Sport in Brazil. With Maradona, he was named by FIFA joint player of the twentieth century.

Below: Pelé in action.

Michel Platini
(France, b. 1955)

Clubs: *Nancy (1972–79),*
Saint Etienne (1979–82), Juventus
(1982–87)
Caps: *72 (41 goals)*

An accomplished, stylish midfielder
with a forward's instinct for goals,
Platini captained France to the top of
European international football in the
1980s. After spending his early years
with Nancy and Saint Etienne (his 20
goals had won the French league for
Saint Etienne in 1982) Platini moved to
Juventus. He scored 16 league goals in
his first season and helped Juventus
reach the European Cup Final, losing
1–0 to Hamburg. In 1984 his goals
helped Juventus win the league and the
Cup Winners Cup. That year, playing
with Tigana and Giresse, he scored
nine goals for France in the European
Championships, and his free kick in
the final helped France beat Spain 2–0.
Platini played in the Heysel European
Cup Final in 1985, and his penalty gave
Juventus a 1–0 win over Liverpool.
He steered France to the semi-final of
the 1986 World Cup, where they were
beaten by West Germany, and he retired
in 1987. Platini was European Footballer
of the Year three times, in 1983, 1984
and 1985, an honour he shares with
Johan Cruyff and Marco Van Basten.

Above: Michel Platini, French captain in the 1984 European Championships, where
he inspired his team-mates to victory in the tournament.

Robert Prosinecki
(West Germany, b. 1969)

Clubs: *Red Star Belgrade*
(1987–91), Real Madrid (1992–94),
Real Oviedo (1994–95), Barcelona
(1995–96), Seville (1996–97),
Croatia Zagreb (1997–2000),
Standard Liege (2000–01),
Portsmouth (2001–)
Caps: *5 (4 goals) Yugoslavia;*
49 (10) Croatia

Born in West Germany to Yugoslavian
parents, Prosinecki is a playmaking
midfielder with flair and subtlety.
He won three league titles with Red

Star, and was a member of the Red
Star Belgrade side that won the 1991
European Cup Final against Marseille.
His performance prompted Real
Madrid to buy him, and he went on to
play for Real Oviedo, Barcelona and
Seville, although his time in Spain was
marred by injury problems. In total, he
has 49 caps, first with Yugoslavia and
then, after the Balkan wars of the early
1990s, with the newly independent
Croatia, with whom he reached the
quarter-finals of Euro '96 and third
place in the 1998 World Cup finals.
He also played in the 2002 finals, and
was the first player to score in World
Cup finals for two different countries.

Above: Prosinecki breaks for Red Star.

Above: Ferenc Puskas lines up for Hungary against England in 1953.

Ferenc Puskas
(Hungary, b. 1927)

Clubs: *Honved (1943–56),*
Real Madrid (1958–66)
Caps: *84 (83 goals) (Hungary),*
4 (Spain)

The stocky Ferenc Puskas was a legendary footballing wizard with a rocket of a left-foot shot. Known as the "Galloping Major", after his time spent with the Hungarian army side Honved, Puskas played in Hungary's 6–3 and 7–1 humiliations of England in 1953 and 1954, and he joined Real Madrid in 1958. Puskas formed an immediate partnership with the equally legendary Alfredo Di Stefano and, fed by winger Paco Gento, the pair terrorized European defences over the next few years. Puskas scored four goals in Real's demolition of Eintracht Frankfurt in the outstanding 1960 European Cup Final, and he had a hat trick in the first 35 minutes of the 1962 final, although Benfica finally came through to win 5–3. Puskas scored 35 goals in his 38 European Cup appearances. He retired in 1966, shortly after Real's sixth European Cup triumph. In his time with the club he had won a total of five Spanish league titles. Puskas took up management after retirement, and he led Panathinaikos to the 1971 European Cup Final, but they lost 1–0 to an emergent Ajax.

Thomas Ravelli
(Sweden, b. 1959)

Clubs: *Oster Vaxjo,*
IFK Gothenburg (1989–97),
Tampa Bay Rowdies (1997–99)
Caps: *143*

Goalkeeper Ravelli is the most-capped player in Swedish history, with a tally of 143 caps. He was first capped in 1981, and was still pacing the goal when Sweden reached the semi-final of the 1992 European Championships (which they lost to Germany). He also played in the 1994 World Cup finals, with Sweden claiming third place after their victory over Bulgaria. In his time with IFK Gothenburg, he won six Swedish league titles, and he moved to the United States, to the Tampa Bay Rowdies, in 1997. Ravelli retired from football in 1999.

Right: Sweden's long-serving goalkeeper, Thomas Ravelli.

Frank Rijkaard
(Surinam, b. 1962)

Clubs: *Ajax (1980–88), Zaragoza*
(1988), AC Milan (1988–93),
Ajax (1993–95)
Caps: *73 (10 goals)*

One of three Dutchmen in Arrigo Sacchi's AC Milan side, Rijkaard was equally adept in midfield and defence. He began his career with Ajax in 1980, and won a European Cup Winners Cup medal with the team in 1987. After disagreements with manager Johan Cruyff, he had a spell with Zaragoza before joining Milan, with whom he won European Cup winner's medals in 1989 and 1990. On the morning of Milan's European Cup Final against Marseille, he announced his decision to leave. Milan were beaten 1–0 and Rijkaard moved back to Ajax. He won another European Cup winner's medal in 1995, when his pass to Kluivert produced the winning goal in Ajax's 1–0 defeat of AC Milan. He played in Holland's 1988 triumph in the European Championships, but was sent off after an altercation with West Germany's Rudi Voller in the 1990 World Cup. Rijkaard retired in 1995 to manage the Dutch national team, but he resigned after Euro 2000 when Holland were beaten in the semi-final in a penalty shoot-out with Italy.

Left: Rijkaard at Euro '88.

Luigi Riva
(Italy, b. 1944)

Clubs: *Legnano (1962–63), Cagliari (1963–76)*
Caps: *42 (35 goals)*

Left-winger Luigi "Gigi" Riva is the highest goal scorer in Italian football. He started his career as a teenager with Legnano. He joined the second division Cagliari in 1963 and played out his entire career with the Sardinian side. It was Riva's goals that helped the club to their only *Serie A* championship, in 1969–70, and that season he scored 21 goals in 28 games. Riva's international debut was against Hungary in 1965, and he played alongside Mazzola and Boninsegna in the 1970 World Cup finals, where his extra-time goal knocked out West Germany in the semi-final. Riva had been key to Italy's success in the quarter- and semi-finals of that tournament, but he could do little to counter Pelé's Brazilian side, and Italy lost 4–1 to the South Americans in the final. In spite of breaking both his legs on the football pitch (fortunately for him, in separate incidents), Riva continued to play professionally until the mid-1970s, although in the end it was as a result of these injuries that he was forced into premature retirement.

Right: Riva lines up with the Azzurri at the World Cup finals of 1970.

Rivaldo, Victor Barbosa Ferreira (Brazil, b. 1972)

Clubs: *Mogi–Mirim (1992–93), Corinthians (1993–94), Palmeiras (1994–96), Deportivo La Coruña, (1996–97), Barcelona (1997–2002), AC Milan (2002–)*
Caps: *69 (33 goals)*

A poor kid from a slum background in Recife, Rivaldo's sublime talents earned him the World Footballer of the Year title in 1999. Starting his career as a 14-year-old with Paulista Santa Cruz, Rivaldo played for several Brazilian clubs before joining Spanish side Deportivo La Coruña in 1996. A left-sided, ball-playing, attacking midfielder, he has a flair for scoring stunning goals, and he notched up 21 of them in his 41 games with Deportivo. In his first season with Barcelona, in 1997, he scored 19 goals, and helped the Catalan club take the Spanish league and Cup "double". The following season he scored 24 goals and Barcelona won the league again. In 1999 he was top scorer in the *Copa America*, and his two goals in the final helped Brazil retain the trophy. He appeared in the World Cup Final of both 1998 and 2002, winning the gold medal in the latter.

Above: Rivaldo's left foot in action for Barcelona.

Gianni Rivera
(Italy, b. 1943)

Clubs: *Alessandria (1958–60),
AC Milan (1960–79)*
Caps: *60 (14 goals)*

A slight, skilful inside-forward, Rivera
had poise, exceptional passing ability
and a powerful shot. A teenage
prodigy, he joined AC Milan from his
home-town club Alessandria in 1960,
at the age of 16. Known as *"Il Bambino
d'Oro"* ("The Golden Boy"), he helped
Milan to two European Cup Final wins
in 1963 and 1969, two Cup Winners'
Cups in 1968 and 1973, and two Italian
league and Cup trophies. Winner of the
European Footballer of the Year award
in 1969, Rivera was capped for his
country 60 times, although he only
came on for the last few minutes
of the 1970 World Cup Final, as a
substitute for Roberto Boninsegna.
On retirement, he became president of
Milan and moved into Italian politics.

*Right: Gianni Rivera, the "Golden Boy"
for Italy and AC Milan, during the
1970 World Cup finals.*

Paolo Rossi
(Italy, b. 1956)

Clubs: *Juventus (1972–75),
Como (1975–76), Lanerossi Vicenza
(1976–79), Perugia (1979–80),
Juventus (1981–85), AC Milan
(1986–86), Verona (1986–87)*
Caps: *48 (20 goals)*

The young forward Rossi was bought
by Juventus in 1972 and loaned out
to various Italian clubs because of a
knee injury that prevented him playing
regular games for the *Serie A* side.
After a fine display for his national side
in the 1978 World Cup finals, where he
scored three goals, Rossi was bought
by Perugia – the provincial club had
outbid the mighty Juventus, who
were now keen to reclaim their

Left: Rossi in the 1982 World Cup finals.

former player. However, because of
his involvement in a betting and bribes
scandal, Rossi was banned from
playing professional football
for three years. The financial
implications of this threatened
to damage Perugia and, eventually,
Juventus bought him back. Rossi
played for Italy in the 1982 World
Cup finals, and was an unexpected
sensation in the tournament, scoring
a hat trick against Brazil in Italy's 3–2
quarter-final win, as well as both goals
in the 2–0 semi-final defeat of Poland,
and the first goal in the 3–1 final
victory against West Germany.
He came away as top scorer of the
tournment, and that year he was
named European Footballer of the
Year. Rossi played briefly for AC Milan
and Verona, but injuries forced his
early retirement from the game, at the
age of 29.

Bryan Robson
(England, b. 1957)

Clubs: *West Bromwich Albion (1974–81), Manchester United (1981–94), Middlesbrough (1994–98)*
Caps: *90 (26 goals)*

Robson was England's most influential midfielder of the 1980s. He was a strong, aggressive player, fast and with a fierce shot, and an inspirational captain with England and Manchester United. He joined United from West Bromwich Albion in 1981 for £1.5 million, and by the end of the decade he had led the club to three FA Cup Final victories. He gained his first cap in 1980 and scored the fastest goal ever, in 27 seconds, in the World Cup finals in 1982. Injury prevented him from playing in all of the 1986 finals games, and he received his last cap in 1991, the same year his United team collected the European Cup Winners Cup, beating Barcelona in the final. United won their first Premier League title in 1993, but Robson was on his way out. He left for Middlesbrough in 1994 as player-manager, remaining manager till 2001.

Above: "Captain Marvel" Bryan Robson takes aim for Manchester United.

Above: Romario, the "bad boy" of Brazilian football, played a starring role at USA '94.

Romario Da Souza Faria
(Brazil, b. 1966)

Clubs: *Vasco Da Gama (1984–88), PSV Eindhoven (1988–93), Barcelona (1993–95), Flamengo (1995–96), Valéncia (1996), Flamengo (1996–98), Vasco Da Gama (1998–)*
Caps: *69 (53 goals)*

The controversial Brazilian striker Romario joined PSV Eindhoven from Vasco Da Gama in 1988. The temperamental star had many run-ins with the Dutch club but by the time he left for Barcelona, in 1993, he had scored 125 goals. The £2.3 million forward scored a hat trick in his first game for Barcelona, and played in the team's 4–0 humiliation by AC Milan in the 1994 European Cup Final. After a period in the international wilderness, he was recalled for the World Cup qualifier, against Uruguay, and he scored the two goals that took Brazil to the 1994 finals. He totalled five goals in that tournament, including the winner against Sweden in the semi-final, and he took home a winner's medal. He returned to Brazil in 1995, had a spell with Valéncia, then went back to Flamengo in 1996. He missed the 1998 World Cup due to injury, but played for Vasco da Gama in the 2000 World Club Championship. Romario was South American Player of the Year in 2000.

Ronaldo Luiz Nazario da Lima (Brazil, b. 1976)

Clubs: *Cruzeiro (1993–94), PSV Eindhoven (1994–96), Barcelona (1996–97), Inter Milan (1997–2002), Real Madrid (2002–)*
Caps: *65 (45 goals)*

Possibly the best-known player in the world, the athletic, lightning-fast Ronaldo is a striker of the highest quality. From Cruzeiro he moved to PSV Eindhoven in 1994, where he scored 35 goals in his first season. He was voted World Footballer of the Year in 1996, and joined Barcelona that year for £13 million. In 1997 he scored the goal that won Barcelona the European Cup Winners Cup, and again picked up the World Footballer of the Year award. Inter Milan paid £18 million for his services in 1997. He won a UEFA Cup winner's medal with them in 1998, but a series of serious injuries restricted his appearances. He scored four goals in the 1998 World Cup finals, but suffered a fit on Final day and played poorly. Everything was put right in 2002, when he top-scored with eight goals, including the only two of the Final, to lead Brazil to triumph. Ronaldo was World Footballer of the Year in 2003.

Right: Brazilian superstar Ronaldo.

Karl-Heinz Rummenigge (Germany, b. 1955)

Clubs: *Bayern Munich (1974–84), Inter Milan (1984–87), Servette (1987–88)*
Caps: *95 (45 goals)*

The young bank clerk Rummenigge joined Bayern Munich from Lippstadt in 1974. Within two years the right-winger had won a European Cup winner's medal, when Bayern beat Saint Etienne in 1976. He made his international debut that year and

Left: Stylish winger Rummenigge.

played in the 1978 World Cup finals, scoring three goals. He also starred in West Germany's 1980 European Championship victory. In 1980 and 1981 Rummenigge was voted European Footballer of the Year. He led West Germany to the World Cup Final in 1982, losing to Italy, and to the final of 1986, where they lost again, this time 3–2 to Argentina. In the 1982 tournament he scored five goals and finished as second top scorer. Inter Milan paid Bayern £2.5 million for Rummenigge in 1984. He left the Italian club in 1987 for one last season with Switzerland's Servette before retiring from the game.

Ian Rush (Wales, b. 1961)

Clubs: *Chester (1978–80), Liverpool (1980–87), Juventus (1987–88), Liverpool (1988–96), Leeds United (1996–97), Sheffield United (1997–98), Newcastle United (1998–2000)*
Caps: *73 (28 goals)*

One of the most prolific strikers in modern English footballing history, Ian Rush spent the bulk of his career with Liverpool, whom he first joined in 1980, at the age of 18. Liverpool paid only £300,000 to secure the purchase of Rush from Chester, and their far-sightedness proved to be one of the great investments of the decade. Rush's goals and his selfless contribution to the team helped Liverpool win four league titles, four League Cups and two European Cups over the next six years. He moved briefly to Juventus, for £3.2 million in 1986, but could not settle with the Italian club, and he returned to Liverpool the following year. He scored twice in the FA Cup Final against Everton in 1989, and picked up a fifth league winner's medal in 1990. He was the all-time top scorer at Anfield, with 336 goals, and he is the highest-ever scorer in the FA Cup with 42 goals. Leeds United wasted no time in signing Rush when Liverpool released him on a free transfer in 1996, but he stayed for only one season before moving across Yorkshire to Sheffield United. He then moved to Newcastle. He currently runs a "finishing school" for strikers.

Right: Liverpool's Ian Rush strides forward towards goal.

Above: The tough, determined German sweeper Matthias Sammer.

Matthias Sammer (Germany, b. 1967)

Clubs: *Dynamo Dresden, VfB Stuttgart, Inter Milan, Borussia Dortmund*
Caps: *23 (6 goals) East Germany, 51 (8 goals) Germany*

A strong, attacking sweeper, Sammer, along with Andreas Thom, was the first East German to play for the newly unified German team in 1990. Apart from a brief spell with Inter Milan, he played in Germany, finally with Borussia Dortmund, whom he captained to a 3–1 European Cup victory over Juventus in 1997. He was in the German side that lost in the final of the European Championship in 1992, but was in the victorious 1996 side, scoring the winner against Croatia in the quarter-final. Sammer was voted European Footballer of the Year in 1996. An injury prevented him from appearing in the 1998 World Cup finals. He took over as coach at Dortmund and in 2002 became the youngest coach in history to win the *Bundesliga* when his side topped the table.

Hugo Sanchez
(Mexico, b. 1958)

Clubs: *UNAM (1976–81),*
Atlectico Madrid (1981–85),
Real Madrid (1985–88),
North America (1988–93),
Rayo Vallecano (1993)
Caps: *57 (26 goals)*

Mexico's star player, Hugo Sanchez was an expert goal scorer, and he celebrated his goals with exuberant somersaults. He was leading scorer with Mexico City's UNAM, and then moved to Real Madrid where he was top scorer in the Spanish league for four consecutive seasons between 1985 and 1988. His goals, with contributions from fellow striker Butragueno, made Real the top Spanish side of the late 1980s, winning the Spanish league for five years in succession. Sanchez played for Mexico in the 1978 World Cup finals and he captained his country as far as the quarter-finals in the 1986 tournament.

Above: Mexico's goal-scoring legend Hugo Sanchez in the 1986 World Cup finals.

Gyorgy Sarosi
(Hungary, 1912–1993)

Clubs: *Ferencvaros (1931–43)*
Caps: *61 (42 goals)*

A complete athlete, Sarosi was also a versatile footballer, and he played in several positions for Ferencvaros and Hungary. Essentially a striker, he could also operate in central defence, and he helped Ferencvaros win five Hungarian league titles between 1932 and 1941. He captained Hungary to the 1938 World Cup finals, where he scored four goals in the tournament, including one in the final to reduce Italy's lead to 3–2, although a Piola goal eventually finished off the Hungarians. After his retirement he moved to Italy, where he managed a number of clubs, including Juventus, Bari and Roma.

Right: Hungarian captain Gyorgy Sarosi (right) before the World Cup Final of 1938.

Dejan Savicevic
(Yugoslavia, b. 1966)

Clubs: *Boducnost Titograd (1982–88), Red Star Belgrade (1988–92), AC Milan (1992–98), Red Star Belgrade (1998–99), Rapid Vienna (1999–2001)*
Caps: *56 (20 goals)*

The talented Yugoslavian midfielder Savicevic played in the Red Star Belgrade side that won the European Cup in 1991, beating Marseille on penalties. He transferred to AC Milan for £4 million in 1992, where his dribbling prowess, confident touch and flair for goals earned him the nickname of "the genius". He was outstanding in Milan's 4–0 defeat of Barcelona in the 1994 European Cup Final, where he scored a memorable goal and collected his second European Cup medal. He left Milan to return to Red Star in 1998, and was appointed club captain, but it was short-lived and he left to join Rapid Vienna in 1999.

Above: Dejan Savicevic (right), for AC Milan, glides through the Barcelona defence in the European Cup Final of 1994.

Juan Schiaffino
(Uruguay, b. 1925)

Clubs: *Penarol (1945–54), AC Milan (1954–60), Roma (1960–62)*
Caps: *45 (Uruguay), 4 (Italy)*

A small but lethal inside-forward, Schiaffino was transferred from Penarol to AC Milan in 1954 for a then world-record fee of £72,000. He scored the opening goal in the 1958 European Cup Final against Real Madrid, although Milan lost 3–2 in extra time. He played for Uruguay in the 1950 World Cup Final, and scored the equalizer against Brazil to help Uruguay win 2–1; Schiaffino provided five goals that tournament. He played again in the 1954 finals, and Uruguay took fourth place. After retirement he returned home to manage Penarol and, in 1975, he was appointed manager of the Uruguay national team.

Above: Juan Schiaffino, Uruguay''s geatest-ever football export.

Peter Schmeichel (Denmark, b. 1963)

Clubs: *Hvidvore (1984–87), Brondby (1987–91), Manchester United (1991–99), Sporting Lisbon (1999–2001), Aston Villa (2001–2), Manchester City (2002–3)*
Caps: *129 (1)*

A massive presence between the goalposts, Schmeichel is an athletic and acrobatic keeper. He won four Danish league titles with Brondby and moved to Manchester United, for £550,000, in 1991. By the time he transferred to Sporting Lisbon in 1999, Schmeichel's stopping ability had helped United to five league titles and a European Cup victory over Bayern Munich in 1999. His talent helped Sporting Lisbon to the Portuguese title in 2000, their first championship victory since 1982. He was first capped

Above: The intimidating, athletic figure of Peter Schmeichel.

in 1987 and his goalkeeping skill, particularly his save from Van Basten's penalty in the semi-final shoot-out against Holland, was instrumental in Denmark's shock success in the 1992 European Championships. He played in Euro '96, and captained Denmark to a quarter-final place in the 1998 World Cup, when they lost to Brazil.

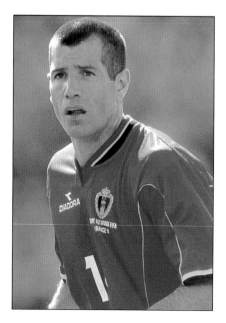

Vicenzo "Enzo" Scifo (Belgium, b. 1966)

Clubs: *Anderlecht (1982–87), Inter Milan (1987–88), Bordeaux (1988–89), Auxerre (1989–91), Torino (1991–93), Monaco (1993–97), Anderlecht (1997–2000)*
Caps: *84 (18)*

One of Belgium's finest-ever players, Scifo made his debut for Anderlecht at the age of 17. His guile and his goals

Left: Enzo Scifo, star of four World Cup tournaments for Belgium.

were behind Anderlecht's three league titles in succession between 1985 and 1987, and he moved to Inter Milan in 1987. He was loaned to French clubs Bordeaux and Auxerre before joining Torino in 1990. Scifo was first capped in 1984, and he played in the 1986 World Cup finals where he guided Belgium to fourth place, losing 2–0 to Argentina in the semi-finals. In the 1990 finals in Italy, he played in the Belgium side that reached the second round but was knocked out by a late David Platt goal for England. Scifo played in the 1998 World Cup finals in France, making his fourth appearance in the tournament. He retired in 2000.

Uwe Seeler
(Germany, b. 1936)

Club: *Hamburg (1953–71)*
Caps: *72 (43 goals)*

Seeler was West Germany's top striker throughout the 1960s, eventually giving way to the young Gerd Müller. The son of a former Hamburg player, Seeler showed a loyalty to Hamburg throughout his professional career – playing his club football only for the north German side and turning down some tempting offers from Italian and Spanish clubs. He was captain when the club were beaten 2–0 by AC Milan in the 1968 Cup Winners' Cup Final. A small but powerful centre-forward,

he captained West Germany to the 1966 World Cup Final, losing 4–2 to England. He also scored a remarkable back-header in the 1970 World Cup finals to equalize against England in the quarter-final, when England threw away a 2–0 lead to lose 3–2. So central was Seeler to German football of the 1960s and early 1970s that the German fans adopted his name for their chant ("Uwe! Uwe!") at international football matches. He shares with Pelé the distinction of having scored in four World Cup finals, in 1958, 1962, 1966 and 1970. Seeler retired in 1971 and eventually became club president of Hamburg.

Right: West German captain, Uwe Seeler.

Alan Shearer
(England, b. 1970)

Clubs: *Southampton (1988–92),*
Blackburn Rovers (1992–96),
Newcastle United (1996–)
Caps: *63 (30 goals)*

A high-scoring striker, Shearer was a teenage sensation with Southampton. At 17, he became the youngest player to score a hat trick in Division One, in Southampton's 4–2 defeat of Arsenal in 1988. He moved to Blackburn in 1992 for £3.6 million. Blackburn won the league title in 1995, with Shearer scoring 34 goals, and in 1996 he became the first player to score more than 30 goals in three successive seasons in the top division. Shearer joined Newcastle for a record figure of £15 million in 1996, making him the world's most expensive player, and his form revived when Bobby Robson became manager, following the departure of Ruud Gullit. He made his international debut in 1992, and in Euro '96 he was top scorer with five goals, including England's opener against Germany in the semi-final. He captained England to the 1998 World Cup finals, scoring twice. Shearer retired from the international game after Euro 2000.

Above: Alan Shearer on the attack for Newcastle United.

Peter Shilton
(England, b. 1949)

Clubs: *Leicester City (1966–74), Stoke City (1974–77), Nottingham Forest (1977–82), Southampton (1982–87), Derby County (1987–92), Plymouth Argyle (1992–95), Wimbledon (1995), Bolton (1995), Coventry (1995–96), West Ham (1996), Leyton Orient (1996–97)*
Caps: *125*

The successor to Gordon Banks as England's goalkeeper, Peter Shilton had a long and illustrious career between the goal posts. After Leicester and Stoke City, Shilton joined Nottingham Forest in 1977 and, under the inspirational Brian Clough, he won two European Cup winner's medals, playing in the side that beat Malmo in 1979 and Hamburg in 1980. He was first capped in 1970 and played in the 1982 World Cup finals, letting in only one goal in five games. He played again in 1986, losing to Argentina and Maradona's infamous "Hand of God" goal in the quarter-final. He played in his last World Cup finals in 1990, when England lost to West Germany in the semi-final. Shilton played his 1000th league match for Leyton Orient in 1996, at the age of 47.

Left: Peter Shilton dives to make a save for Nottingham Forest.

Omar Sivori
(Argentina, b. 1935)

Clubs: *River Plate (1952–57), Juventus (1957–65), Napoli (1965–69), River Plate (1969)*
Caps: *18 (9 goals) (Argentina), 9 (8 goals) (Italy)*

Playing alongside the big Welshman John Charles in the Juventus attack, Omar Sivori was a fiery inside-left with abundant skills and a sharp eye for goal. He began his career with River Plate and won three Argentinian league titles in succession between 1955 and 1957. After starring in the 1957 *Copa America*, Sivori moved to Juventus for a record £91,000, and his two goals brought Juventus the Italian league three times in 1958, 1960 and 1961. He was voted European Footballer of the Year in 1961. He joined Napoli in 1965, having scored nearly 150 goals for Juventus, and he became manager of the Argentinian national team in 1973.

Right: Juventus' Argentinian forward, Omar Sivori.

Socrates
(Brazil, b. 1954)

Clubs: *Botafogo (1974–76), Corinthians (1977–84), Fiorentina (1984–85), Flamengo (1985–87), Santos (1988–90)*
Caps: *60 (22 goals)*

The bearded Socrates, a qualified doctor, was a stylish midfielder who captained Brazil in the 1982 and 1986 World Cup finals. He played first with Botafogo as an amateur and, after collecting his medical degree, joined Corinthians as a professional in 1977. In 1982 he took Brazil to the World Cup quarter-final, having scored a brilliant goal against the Soviet Union, but despite scoring, his team lost to the eventual champions, Italy. In 1986 Brazil reached the semi-final but lost on penalties to France, with Socrates missing his first attempt. He played his club football in Brazil, moving without success to Fiorentina for one season in 1984, before rounding off his career with Santos.

Right: Brazilian captain Socrates during the 1982 World Cup quarter-final.

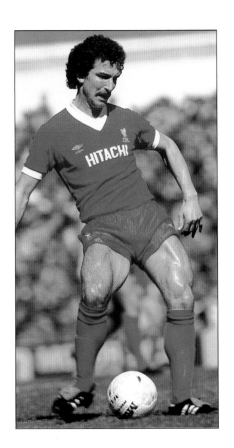

Graeme Souness
(Scotland, b. 1953)

Clubs: *Tottenham Hotspur (1968–73), Middlesbrough (1973–78), Liverpool (1978–84), Sampdoria (1984–86), Rangers (1986–91)*
Caps: *54 (3 goals)*

The tough-tackling, intimidating Souness was also a skilful and perceptive midfielder with Liverpool and Scotland. He joined Liverpool from Middlesbrough in 1978 and played in the 1978 European Cup Final, making Dalglish's winning goal. As captain of the side, he played in two further European Cup Finals with Liverpool, winning both, then moved on to the

Left: Graeme Souness, Liverpool's midfield enforcer.

Italian side Sampdoria in 1984, having played over 350 games for the Reds. Despite becoming a favourite with the fans at the Genovese club, Souness made his return to British football in 1986, as player-manager of Rangers. He was the first Rangers manager ever to sign a Catholic (Mo Johnston), and under his stewardship the Glasgow side won their first league title for nine years. He represented Scotland in three World Cup finals, 1978, 1982 and 1986, and played his last international in 1986. Souness left Rangers in 1991 to become manager of Liverpool – taking over from his friend and former team-mate Kenny Dalglish. The appointment was less successful, however, and Souness stayed for less than three seasons at the Anfield ground. His managerial career has since included spells at Galatasaray, Southampton, Benfica and Blackburn Rovers.

Hristo Stoichkov
(Bulgaria, b. 1966)

Clubs: *CSKA Sofia (1984–90), Barcelona (1990–95), Parma (1995–96), Barcelona (1996–98), CSKA Sofia (1998–99), Chicago Fire (2000–)*
Caps: *83*

Centre-forward Stoichkov is a Bulgarian national hero. He began his career with CSKA Sofia, and was bought by Barcelona for £2 million in 1990, after securing three Bulgarian league winner's medals. He scored 60 goals in his first three years with Barcelona, and played in two European Cup Finals, when they beat Sampdoria in 1992 and lost to AC Milan two years later. He first played for Bulgaria in 1987, and his six goals in the 1994 World Cup finals made him the leading scorer and took Bulgaria to the semi-finals, beating the holders Germany along the way. Stoichkov also played in Euro '96 and the 1998 World Cup finals, but this time Bulgaria did not impress. He left Barcelona for a season with Parma, but returned in 1996 and went back to CSKA in 1998. He retired from international football in 1999, after a friendly with England. Stoichkov ended his club football in Japan, Saudi Arabia and the United States.

Above: The voluble Hristo Stoichkov, captain and hero of the Bulgarian national team and goal-scoring machine for Barcelona.

Luis Suarez
(Spain, b. 1935)

Clubs: *Deportivo La Coruña (1951–53), Barcelona (1953–61), Inter Milan (1961–70), Sampdoria (1970–73)*
Caps: *32 (14 goals)*

Midfield general Suarez was one of Spain's greatest players. The slim, tricky player left Deportivo La Coruña in 1954 for Barcelona, and played in Barcelona's 3–2 European Cup Final defeat by Benfica, in 1962. He was voted European Footballer of the Year in 1960, and he moved to Inter Milan for a then world record transfer fee of £150,000 in 1962. His dominance of the midfield area, perceptive passing and explosive shot led Inter Milan to two European Cup victories in 1963 and 1964. Suarez missed playing in Inter's 2–1 defeat by Celtic in the 1967 European Cup Final due to injury. He helped Spain to their European Championship victory in 1964, and played in the 1966 World Cup finals in England. Suarez retired as a player after a spell in Italy with Sampdoria, and he took over the role of Spain's national manager in 1989. He led the team to the second round in the 1990 World Cup finals, having finished top of their group section.

Left: Luis Suarez in the blue and black stripes of Inter Milan.

Davor Suker
(Croatia, b. 1968)

Clubs: *FC Osijek (1985–89).
Dynamo Zagreb (1989–91), Seville
(1991–96), Real Madrid (1996–99),
Arsenal (1999–2000), West Ham
United (2000–01), 1860 Munich
(2001–)*
Caps: *69 (45 goals)*

Suker is Croatia's greatest-ever striker,
and the national team's leading goal
scorer. He moved from Dynamo
Zagreb to Seville in 1991, and then
on to Real Madrid in 1996. He helped
Real win the Spanish league in 1997,
and came on as a last-minute substitute
in their European Cup Final victory
over Juventus in 1998. Suker made
his international debut for the former
Yugoslavia in 1990, and he scored
a famous goal in Euro '96 when he
cheekily chipped the ball over the
retreating Peter Schmeichel. In the
1998 World Cup finals, Suker was the
top scorer with six goals, and his goal
in the play-off against Holland helped
Croatia claim third place. He also
played in the 2002 World Cup finals.
At club level, he lost his place in the
Real side to Fernando Morientes, and
since 1999 he has played for Arsenal,
West Ham and 1860 Munich.

Right: Davor Suker playing for Arsenal.

Marco Van Basten
(Holland, b. 1964)

Clubs: *Ajax (1981–87),
AC Milan (1987–95)*
Caps: *58 (24 goals)*

A tall, gifted striker, Van Basten was
a prolific goal-scoring forward for
Ajax, Milan and Holland in the 1980s
and early 1990s. He made his debut
for Ajax as a teenager, coming on as
substitute for Johann Cruyff, and he
lifted three Dutch league titles and
scored 128 league goals in his five
years at the club. Bought by AC Milan
in 1987 for £1.5 million, his goals
helped Silvio Berlusconi's team win
two European Cups in succession,
in 1989 and 1990. He played in
Holland's triumphant 1988 European
Championship, and scored a brilliant
20-yard volley against the USSR in
the final. He was named European
Footballer of the Year in 1988, 1989
and 1992, and World Footballer of the
Year in 1988 and 1992. He played in the
1993 European Cup Final, losing 1–0 to
Marseille, but a series of injuries forced
him to end his career at the age of 30.
He had scored an outstanding tally of
90 goals in 147 games for Milan.

*Left: Marco Van Basten, arguably the
finest striker of all time.*

Carlos Valderrama
(Colombia, b. 1961)

Clubs: *Millionarios (1984–85), Atlético Nacional (1985–88), Montpellier (1988–91), Real Valladolid (1991–92), Atlético National (1992–93), Atlético Junior (1993–96), Tampa Bay Mutiny (1996–97), Miami Fusion (1997–98), Tampa Bay Mutiny (1999)*
Caps: *111 (10 goals)*

Identified by his mane of frizzy, orange hair, midfielder Valderrama represented Colombia in six consecutive *Copa America* competitions, between 1987 and 1997, and in the World Cup finals of 1990, 1994 and 1998. He made his international debut in 1985 against Paraguay, and was voted South American Player of the Year in 1987 and 1994. In 1990 he helped take Colombia to the second round of the World Cup finals, but he could do nothing about Andres Escobar's own goal against the USA in 1994, and Colombia were knocked out. He played at France '98 at the age of 38.

Above: The frizzy haired Carlos Valderrama, the inspiration behind Colombia.

Above: Paul Van Himst (right) crosses the ball past the lunging Franz Beckenbauer.

Paul Van Himst
(Belgium, b. 1943)

Clubs: *Anderlecht (1959–75), RWD Molenbeek, Enndracht Aalst*
Caps: *81 (31 goals)*

Centre-forward Van Himst was a young footballing prodigy, playing his first game for RSC Anderlecht at the tender age of 16. In his time at the club, he achieved eight Belgian league title winner's medals, between 1962 and 1974, and was the league's top scorer three times. He represented Belgium at the 1970 World Cup finals. On his retirement he managed Anderlecht and then took over as Belgium's coach, leading the country to the 1982 World Cup finals, where they reached the second round, and was also in charge for the 1994 finals. He was recently voted Belgium's Footballer of the Century.

Juan Sebastian Verón
(Argentina, b. 1975)

Clubs: *Estudiantes (1992–96), Boca Juniors (1996), Sampdoria (1996–98), Parma (1998–99), Lazio (1999–2001), Manchester United (2001–3), Chelsea (2003–)*
Caps: *50 (8 goals)*

A strong, inventive midfielder, Verón followed in his father footsteps by joining Estudiantes in 1992. He helped the club to promotion to the Argentine First Division, and joined Boca Juniors in 1996, where he was idolized by the Buenos Aires fans. Italy was next and he played for Sampdoria for two years before transferring to Parma, with whom he won the UEFA Cup in 1999. That summer he joined Lazio for £18 million, and they reached the quarter-final of the European Cup where, in spite of his magnificent strike, they were eliminated by Valéncia. In 2001 he joined Manchester United for £28 million, but after a mediocre two years, he was sold to Chelsea in 2003 for £15 million. Having made his international debut for Argentina in 1996, Verón is now a mainstay in midfield for his country, and he played in the teams that reached the World Cup quarter-final in 1998 and disappointed in the 2002 finals.

Right: Juan Verón in the 1998 World Cup finals in France.

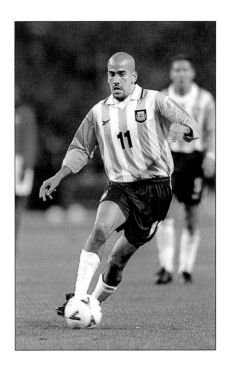

Gianluca Vialli
(Italy, b. 1964)

Clubs: *Cremonese (1980–84), Sampdoria (1984–92), Juventus (1992–96), Chelsea (1996–1999)*
Caps: *59 (16 goals)*

Born into a wealthy family in Cremona, northern Italy, striker Vialli joined his local club Cremonese in 1980 and moved to Sampdoria in 1984. Striking up a partnership with fellow forward Roberto Mancini, he helped his club to the 1990 Cup Winners' Cup Final, scoring both goals in their 2–0 win against Anderlecht. His last game for Sampdoria was the 1992 European Cup Final, when they lost 1–0 to Barcelona. He won the UEFA Cup again in 1993 with Juventus, and won the European Cup, as captain, in 1996, defeating Ajax on penalties. He joined Chelsea in 1996 and was appointed player-manager in 1998, following the departure of Ruud Gullit. In his first season, he led his club to the Cup Winners' Cup Final, when they beat Stuttgart 1–0 to claim the trophy, and two years later his team won the 2000 FA Cup Final. He became manager of Watford for a season in 2001.

Left: Luca Vialli represents his country.

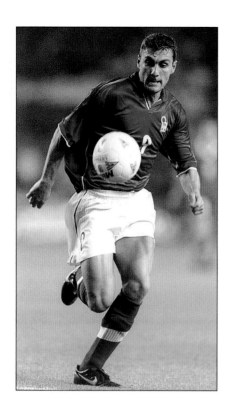

Christian Vieri
(Italy, b. 1973)

Clubs: *Prato (1989–90), Torino (1990–92), Ravena (1993–94), Venezia (1994–95), Atalanta (1995–96), Juventus (1996–97), Atlético Madrid (1997–98), Lazio (1998–99), Inter Milan (1999–)*
Caps: *29 (16 goals)*

Vieri is a big, strong, classic centre-forward and an excellent header of the ball. He set the record for the world's most expensive player (which has since been broken by Zinedine Zidane) when he moved from Lazio to Inter Milan in the summer of 1999 for

Left: Christian Vieri, briefly the world's most expensive player in 1999.

£32 million. He has had something of a peripatetic career to date. He made his *Serie A* debut in 1991 in a 2–0 Torino win against Fiorentina, and played for four other Italian clubs before being transferred from Juventus (whom he represented in the 1997 European Cup Final) to Atlético Madrid in the summer of that year. He scored 24 goals in his season with the Spanish side, but a disagreement with coach Arrigo Sacchi saw him join Lazio in 1998, and he was top scorer in the year he spent with them. He scored a hat trick on his debut for Inter, but missed much of the season due to injury. Vieri made his international debut in 1997 against Moldova, and he was second top scorer in the 1998 World Cup finals in France. He also played in the 2002 finals.

George Weah
(Liberia, b. 1966)

Clubs: *Tonerre Yaounde (1986–88), Monaco (1988–92), Paris Saint–Germain (1992–95), AC Milan (1995–2000), Chelsea (2000), Manchester City (2000)*
Caps: *61 (22)*

Weah is the most respected man in Liberia, not only for his football skills, but also for his financial help and commitment to that war-torn country. A tall centre-forward with exceptional ball control and the ability to score explosive goals, he left Liberia in 1988 to join Monaco, who won the French league in 1991. In the 1995 European Cup he was tournament top scorer, with eight goals for PSG, and was voted European Footballer of the Year. He was four times African Footballer of the Year in 1989 and 1994 to 1996; he crowned this with the World Footballer of the Year award in 1996. Weah moved to AC Milan in 1995 and picked up two *Serie A* winner's medals. After short spells in England and the United Arab Emirates, he announced his retirement in 2002. He lives in New York and is a UNICEF ambassador.

Above: George Weah, Africa's finest player in the 1990s.

Billy Wright
(England, 1924–1994)

Clubs: *Wolverhampton Wanderers (1941–59)*
Caps: *105 (3 goals)*

Wright was a solid and dependable defender, and captain of Wolves and England throughout the 1950s. He was a quiet but inspirational captain, with a precise tackle and effective heading and passing skills. He was centre-half in the Wolves side that won three league titles in the 1950s, under manager Stan Cullis, playing their robust, long-ball game. He was first capped in 1946, and played in the 1950, 1954 and 1958 World Cup finals. He received his record one hundredth cap in a game against Scotland in 1959. He retired in 1959 and was awarded the CBE that year. He became manager of Arsenal in 1962, but left Highbury in 1966 to pursue a media career. He came back to Wolves as a director of the club in 1990. Wright died in 1994.

Above: Wolves captain Billy Wright (right) clears the ball.

Lev Yashin
(Soviet Union, 1929–1990)

Clubs: *Moscow Dynamo (1949–70)*
Caps: *78*

Known as the "Black Panther" in Europe because of his distinctive all-black strip, Lev Yashin is widely regarded as the best goalkeeper in the history of football. His whole career was spent with Moscow Dynamo; he made his debut in 1951 and won five Soviet league winner's medals. He gained his first cap in 1954, won an Olympic gold in 1956 and played in the 1958 World Cup finals. With Yashin in goal, the Soviet Union won the inaugural European Championships in 1960. Yashin then played in the 1962 World Cup finals, but he made some uncharacteristic errors and the Soviets' lost in the quarter-final to Chile. He was in goal for the international FIFA side, the "Rest of the World", against England in 1963, and in that year he became the only goalkeeper ever to be made European Footballer of the Year. In 1966 another error by Yashin in the World Cup allowed Franz Beckenbauer to score the winning goal in the semi-final, although the Russian had a good tournament. Yashin was awarded the Order of Lenin in 1968 as an honour from the Soviet government, and when he retired in 1970, the event was marked with a testimonial match at the Lenin stadium in Moscow, in front of 100,000 fans. Yashin was held in such high regard by the world of football that players such as Pelé, Eusebio and Franz Beckenbauer all travelled to the Soviet Union for the game. Yashin continued to be involved with football after his playing days had ended, and he became manager of Moscow Dynamo in 1971. He died in 1990.

Right: Lev Yashin, the best goalkeeper in footballing history.

Zico, Artur Antunes Coimbra (Brazil, b. 1953)

Clubs: *Flamengo (1970–83), Udinese (1983–85), Flamengo (1985–92), Kashima Antlers (1992)*
Caps: *66 (45 goals)*

Known as the "White Pelé", Zico is Brazil's second-highest goal scorer after the master. The wiry forward played in the 1978 World Cup finals and thought he had scored the winning goal against Sweden, but referee Clive Thomas blew his whistle for full time while the ball was in mid-air, between Zico and the back of the net. Zico played again in the 1982 and 1986 tournaments. It was his 11 goals in South America's *Copa Libertadores* that helped Flamengo to win the title in 1981. After the 1982 World Cup finals Zico moved to Italy's Udinese. He was voted World Footballer of the Year in 1983, and he returned to Flamengo in 1985. He retired from professional football in 1992 and became Brazil's Sports Minister before moving to Japan a year later, to the Kashima Antlers, to help establish the new J–League. Zico was Brazil's assistant coach at the 1998 World Cup finals.

Above: The "white Pelé" Zico (left) shoots.

Above: The talents of Zinedine Zidane brought him the awards of World and European Footballer of the Year in 1998 and World Footballer of the Year in 2000.

Zinedine Zidane (France, b. 1972)

Clubs: *Cannes (1988–92), Bordeaux (1992–96), Juventus (1996–2001), Real Madrid (2001–)*
Caps: *82 (21 goals)*

A midfielder with tight ball control, perceptive passing talents and a thunderous shot, Zidane is the finest French footballer of his generation. The son of Algerian parents, he moved from Cannes to Bordeaux in 1992. In 1996 he moved to Juventus, and helped them to two consecutive European Cup Finals, although they lost both. Zidane made his first appearance for France in 1994, and was an inspiration as they won the 1998 World Cup. Against Brazil, Zidane headed in two of the goals that won the final 3–0 for the French, and he became a national hero immediately. His abilities were recognized in 1998 when he was voted both European and World Footballer of the Year. Zidane's electrifying performances at Euro 2000 were a crucial contribution to France's triumph in the tournament and he was again elected World Footballer of the Year. In 2001 he was transferred to Real Madrid for a world record £47.2 million, and scored a great winning goal in the 2002 Champions League Final against Bayer Leverkusen.

Dino Zoff
(Italy, b. 1942)

Clubs: *Udinese, Mantova, Napoli (1967–72), Juventus (1972–83)*
Caps: *113*

Zoff was probably Italy's finest-ever goalkeeper. The most-capped Italian keeper of all time, with 113 appearances for his country, he had spells with Udinese, Mantova and Napoli before joining Juventus, in 1972, at the age of 30, where he became the automatic choice in goal.

Left: Dino Zoff makes sure his defence is in order.

Zoff helped Juventus win the UEFA Cup in 1977 (beating Athletic Bilbao on away goals) and the Italian league six times, and he captained Italy to their World Cup triumph in 1982. As the Juventus manager, he won the UEFA Cup again in 1990, and then moved to Lazio in an administrative role. Zoff replaced Cesare Maldini as the manager of the Italian national team, after some disappointing performances from Maldini's side in the 1998 World Cup finals. He took Italy all the way to the final of the European Championships in 2000, but defeat by France, and some vociferous public criticism, led to his prompt resignation and his replacement by Giovanni Trapattoni.

Andoni Zubizarreta
(Spain, b. 1961)

Clubs: *Alaves (1979–81), Athletic Bilbao (1981–86), Barcelona (1986–94), Valéncia (1994–99)*
Caps: *126*

The Basque-born goalkeeper Zubizarreta holds the record for the highest number of Spanish international appearances, with 126 caps. He began his career with his home club, Alaves, and joined Athletic Bilbao in 1981, gaining his first cap in 1985. He joined Barcelona the following year and played in the World Cup finals, losing to Belgium in a quarter-final penalty shoot-out. He played again in the 1990 tournament, and was a member of the Barcelona side that won the 1992 European Cup. However, he let in four goals against AC Milan in the 1994 European Cup Final, and he left the club soon after, on a free transfer, to join Valéncia. He played in two more World Cup finals, in 1994, when Spain were eliminated by Italy in the quarter-final, and again, in 1998, when they failed to qualify from the group stage.

Right: Spanish goalkeeper Andoni Zubizarreta dives to prevent a goal.

The Great Teams

When gifted individual players with complementary skills work together, the result can be sublime. Here we look at some unforgettable dream teams.

Italy, 1934–38

Honours: *World Cup winners 1934, 1938; Olympic Champions, 1936*

In 1934, Mussolini's Italy hosted the World Cup finals. Under manager Vittorio Pozzo, they had exploited the "Orundi" (Argentinians of Italian descent), and three of the team, including captain Luisito Monti, were technically Argentinian. Their great forwards Giuseppe Meazza and Giovanni Ferrari played in the finals, and the team defeated the USA 7–1, Spain 1–0 in a second-round replay and Austria 1–0 to reach the Final against Czechoslovakia. Although the Czechs took the lead, Angelo Schiavo's extra-time goal won the World Cup for the host nation. In 1936 they won the Olympics, beating Austria 2–1 in the final, and in 1938 they went to France for the World Cup finals. Of the 1934 team only Ferrari and Meazza played in the tournament. Silvio Paolo's late goal

Above: Italy's captain Guiseppe Meazza is led off the pitch after Italy beat Spain in the World Cup finals of 1934.

saw off Norway, and he scored two more against France to win 3–1. Against Brazil in the semi-final a penalty from Meazza proved the winner in a 2–1 victory. Italy took on Hungary in the final where a determined performance by Italy was too much for a Gyorgy Sarosi-inspired Hungary, and a Piola goal towards the end saw Italy claim the World Cup for the second time in succession.

Hungary, 1952–56

Honours: *Olympic Champions, 1952, World Cup runners-up, 1954*

The "Mighty Magyars", featuring Zoltan Czibor, Sandor Kocsis, Nandor Hidegkuti and Ferenc Puskas were the most feared side in Europe in the early 1950s. They won the 1952 Olympics and came to Wembley to play England in a friendly match in 1953. They astonished England by giving them a 6–3 football lesson, England's first defeat by a foreign side at home; further humiliation followed six months later with a 7–1 hammering in Budapest. In the 1954 World Cup, Hungary won their quarter-final against Brazil 4–2. The game was known as the "Battle of Berne" as three players were sent off and a mass brawl occurred after the match. In the semi-final Hungary met Uruguay. The game was 2–2 in extra time until Kocsis scored twice for a 4–2 win. In the final against West Germany, the score was 2–2 after only 18 minutes. Hungary piled on the pressure, but Germany scored the winner with six minutes to go. Hungary had failed to win the trophy their talent demanded, and the side was to disintegrate in the wake of the Hungarian Revolution of 1956, as its key players left for the West.

Below: Hungary celebrate another goal in their 1953 6–3 thrashing of England.

Benfica, 1960–69

Honours: *European Cup winners, 1961, 1962; Portuguese Champions 1959–60, 1960–1, 1962–3, 1963–4, 1964–5, 1966–7, 1968–9; Portuguese Cup winners 1962, 1964, 1969*

The Hungarian Bela Guttmann coached Benfica to outstanding success in Europe in the early 1960s. The club broke the stranglehold of Real Madrid and, with such players as midfielder Mario Coluña, striker José Aguas and goalkeeper Costa Pereira, they won the European Cup in 1961, beating Barcelona 3–2. With the brilliant Eusebio now leading the attack, Benfica won the trophy again in 1962, beating Real Madrid 5–3, with the two winning goals coming from Eusebio. Without Guttman, Benfica reached their third final in 1963 against Milan at Wembley. Eusebio scored in the eighteenth minute with a fine solo goal but Brazilian forward José Altafini pulled back two in the second half to give Milan a 2–1 victory. Two years later Benfica were again in the final, but a defensive performance by Inter Milan in the San Siro saw them defeated 1–0. The team, with Eusebio still in attack, played their fifth final of the decade in 1968 and lost again, this time to Manchester United and three extra-time goals. The Benfica team was now an ageing one and their glorious period had come to an end.

England, 1966

Honours: *World Cup winners, 1966*

Alf Ramsey was appointed England manager in 1963 and appointed Bobby Moore as captain. Over the next three years he added Gordon Banks in goal, Ray Wilson and George Cohen as full-backs, with Jackie Charlton in the central defensive role. Alan Ball and Martin Peters controlled midfield with Bobby Charlton and his Manchester United teammate Nobby Stiles, while

upfront toiled Jimmy Greaves and Roger Hunt. In the 1966 World Cup, England began with a disappointing 0–0 draw with Uruguay, but won their next two matches, against Mexico and France, 2–0. Geoff Hurst, who had replaced the injured Greaves, scored the winner in a bad-tempered quarter-final against Argentina, and in the semi-final, Bobby Charlton's two goals were too much for Eusebio's Portugal. Against West Germany in the final on 30 July at Wembley, where England had played all their games, Helmut Haller scored first but Hurst and then Peters made the score 2–1. In the last minute Wolfgang Weber scored to take the game into extra time, where a hotly disputed Hurst goal and then a 20-yard effort for his hat trick gave England their first and only World Cup triumph.

Celtic, 1967

Honours: *European Cup winners, 1967*

Jock Stein had taken over as Celtic manager in 1965 and set about transforming the fortunes of the club. Rangers had been dominant in Scottish football since 1960 but Stein's fast,

Above: English heroes Nobby Stiles, Bobby Moore, Geoff Hurst and Martin Peters with the 1966 World Cup trophy.

exciting side had won the league title for the first time in 12 years. Big Billy McNeill was captain and centre-half, and Jimmy Johnstone chief tormentor on the right wing, while Bobby Murdoch and Bertie Auld schemed in midfield. Steve Chalmers and Bobby Lennox were the chief scorers. The club made its first appearance in the European Cup in 1966–67, knocking out FC Zürich 5–0, Nantes 6–2 and Vjvodina Novi Sad 2–1 in the quarter-final, thanks to a McNeill headed winner. Two goals from Chalmers helped finish off Dukla Prague 3–1 in the semi-final, and Celtic were through to meet Inter Milan in Lisbon in the final. Although Sandro Mazzola scored first for Inter, a screamer of a goal from attacking left-back Tommy Gemmell equalized. With seven minutes left, Chalmers touched in a Murdoch cross, and Celtic became the first British club to win the European Cup. Celtic went on to win a further eight league titles and seven Scottish Cups under Stein, but this was the club's finest moment.

Manchester United, 1968

Honours: *European Cup winners, 1968*

Matt Busby's great Manchester United team, featuring George Best, Denis Law and Bobby Charlton, had reached the semi-final of the European Cup in 1966, only to lose 2–1 to Partizan Belgrade. They were back in 1968, having won the English League, and they dispatched Hibernians Malta and Sarajevo in the opening rounds. Best and a young Brian Kidd both scored against Gornik Zabrze at Old Trafford and Gornik could only score one in Poland. United now had to meet Real Madrid in the semi-final. A Best goal at Old Trafford gave them a 1–0 lead to take to the Bernabeu. With 18 minutes to go, Real were 3–1 ahead on the night but a David Sadler goal and Foulkes' conversion of a Best cross, with just five minutes remaining, scraped United through to face Benfica in the final at Wembley. Charlton opened the scoring and Graca equalized towards the end of normal time. In extra time, a goal from Best and one each from Kidd and Charlton made the final score 4–1. Manchester United were the first English team to lift the European Cup.

Ajax, 1971–73

Honours: *European Cup winners 1971, 1972, 1973; Dutch league champions: 71–72, 72–73; Dutch Cup winners 1971, 1972*

The authoritarian Ajax manager Rinus Michels had discovered the brilliant young forward Johan Cruyff and had designed the philosophy of "total football" around him. Also in his exciting side were the midfielders Johan Neeskens and Arie Haan, winger Piet Keizer, attacking full-back Ruud Krol and the youngster Johnny Rep. The club had reached the 1969 European Cup Final, losing 4–1 to an experienced AC Milan team, but they were back in the final in 1971. Centre-forward Dick Van Dijk and Haan both scored in Ajax's 2–0 defeat of Panathinaikos. The next season, with Stefan Kovacs having taken over from Barcelona-bound Michels, they again reached the final, against Inter Milan. Cruyff scored after a defensive error and then made it 2–0 with a header, and only some stout goalkeeping saved Inter from a much higher scoreline. In 1972–73, a 4–0 thrashing of Bayern Munich in the quarter-final and two wins over Real Madrid in the semis took Ajax through to their third successive final, against Juventus. Johnny Rep scored the winning goal in the sixth minute in what proved a disappointing game, but Ajax had now won the European Cup three times in succession, the first team to do so since Real Madrid. The departure of Cruyff and Neeskens to Barcelona took the heart out of the side; they would not win the European Cup again until 1995.

Below: Ajax's Johnny Rep (front) celebrates after scoring against Juve in the 1973 European Cup Final.

Bayern Munich, 1974–76

Honours: *European Cup winners 1974, 1975, 1976; West German league champions 1973–74*

West German and Bayern Munich captain Franz Beckenbauer was the mastermind behind Bayern's three-year reign as European champions in the 1970s. The attacking sweeper led a team of German internationals, including Gerd Müller, Paul Breitner, Sepp Maier, Uli Hoeness and Georg Schwarzenbeck, and they were a formidable side in the European Cup. They claimed their first trophy in 1974, beating Atlético Madrid 4–1 in a replay. In 1975 they won a toughly contested final against Leeds United. In the 1975–76 tournament Müller scored twice in Bayern's 5–0 crushing of Benfica in the quarter-final, and twice in the semi-final against Real Madrid. Bayern, now with a young Karl-Heinz Rummenigge in the first team, faced Saint Etienne in the final, and a goal from Franz Roth gave Bayern their third European Cup. As with Ajax three years previously, the star players then began to leave. It took until 2001 for Bayern to regain the European Cup.

Liverpool, 1974–83

Honours: *European Cup winners 1977, 1978, 1981; UEFA Cup winners 1976; League title winners 1975–76, 1976–77, 1978–79, 1979–80, 1981–2, 1982–3, 1983–4; FA Cup winners 1974; League Cup winners 1981, 1982, 1983*

The managership of Bob Paisley brought Liverpool more major honours than any other club in the British game. Inheriting Bill Shankly's squad, he shrewdly added to it with the acquisition of Kenny Dalglish, Graeme Souness and Alan Hansen, and he had the finest club in European football for almost a decade. Aside from their many domestic honours, Liverpool won three European Cups under his guidance. In 1977, they beat Borussia Mönchengladbach 3–1 in a thrilling match; the next year, in a less than exciting final against Bruges, Dalglish's delicate chip proved the difference between the two sides; and in 1981 defender Alan Kennedy scored the only goal against Real Madrid. Liverpool won seven league titles during Paisley's reign, three in succession between 1982 and 1984, and they won the League Cup three times between 1981 and 1983. Paisley left the club before Liverpool's victory in the 1984 European Cup Final against Roma, but his astute buying of players included keeper Bruce Grobbelaar and Ian Rush, both of whom would play their parts in the 1984 European campaign.

AC Milan, 1988–94

Honours: *European Cup winners 1989, 1990, 1994; Italian league champions 1987–88, 1991–92, 1992–93, 1993–94*

Millionaire-businessman Silvio Berlusconi bought the debt-ridden, sleeping giant AC Milan in 1986, and he had turned the club into the best in Europe within just three years.

Above: Souness, Dalglish and Hansen, Liverpool's heroes of the 1970s and 80s.

Berlusconi bought three hugely talented Dutchmen, Ruud Gullit, Marco Van Basten and Frank Rijkaard, who lined up alongside classy defenders Franco Baresi and Paolo Maldini, and Roberto Donadoni in midfield. Berlusconi also hired coach Arrigo Sacchi, and in 1988, Milan won their first *Serie A* title for nine years. The following season, they won the European Cup – Gullit and Van Basten both scoring twice in their 4–0 defeat of Steaua Bucharest. In 1990 they won again with a 1–0 victory over Benfica. Sacchi left to run the Italian national side and former player Fabio Capello took over. Milan won the *Serie A* three times from 1992 to 1994, but lost the 1993 European Cup Final 1–0 to Marseille. By 1994 Van Basten had retired but Capello had bought "the genius" Dejan Savicevic and Gianluigi Lentini. Milan reached the European Cup Final that year against Barcelona. In an outstanding performance from the Italians, they humbled Barcelona 4–0, with Daniele Massaro scoring a hat trick and Savicevic scoring one. However, a decline then set in, and Milan lost the 1995 final to a youthful Ajax side.

Juventus, 1994–98

Honours: *European Cup winners 1996; Italian league champions 1994–95, 1996–97, 1997–98*

When coach Marcello Lippi took over the venerable old club Juventus in 1994, he already had in the side such quality players as Gianluca Vialli, Fabrizio Ravanelli, Roberto Baggio, the young Alessandro Del Piero, Paulo Sousa and Didier Deschamps. They won their first *Serie A* title for nine years in 1994–5, and reached the European Cup Final the following year to play Ajax. Ravanelli scored an early goal for Juventus, then Jari Litmanen equalized, but Juventus won in a penalty shoot-out. In 1996–7, now with Christian Vieri, Alen Boksic and French playmaker Zinedine Zidane, Juve won the *Serie A* title, but lost the European Cup Final 3–1 to an unfancied Borussia Dortmund. Lippi's team won the League again in 1997–8, with new striker Filippo Inzaghi and midfielder Edgar Davids, and they knocked out Kiev Dynamo and Monaco to reach their third European Cup Final, this time against Real Madrid. A Predrag Mijatovic-strike sealed the game for Real, and the next season Lippi was sacked. Juventus, however, will be back.

The Great Games

"To say that these men paid their shillings to watch 22 hirelings kick a ball is merely to say that a violin is wood and catgut, that Hamlet is so much paper and ink."
J.B. Priestley in *The Good Companions*, 1929.

Whether or not football is a game that has entertainment as its primary objective is something about which there is much disagreement. To some, it is "the beautiful game", a spectacle that should aim to lift the sprits of the dourest of souls, while to others, any pleasure derived by those watching is no more than a fortunate by-product of an activity that is essentially for the benefit of its participants. Whatever its driving force, and whether by accident or design, the game of football is undoubtedly capable of creating engaging drama of which any script-writer would be proud. To illustrate the round ball's ability to both surprise and entertain we have selected five of the most memorable matches in footballing history.

Below: Real Madrid v Eintracht Frankfurt, arguably the most entertaining game ever played.

Great Upset

United States 1 England 0
29 June 1950, Belo Horizonte, World Cup finals

A classic David and Goliath tale. England, with Finney, Mortensen, Mannion and Wright, took to the field with a record of 22 wins in their 28 games since World War Two. The USA had no international pedigree and their star player was captain Eddie McIlvenny, a Scotsman from Third Division Wrexham. A bumpy pitch, a hostile crowd, the effects of a long domestic season, a touch of arrogance and a headed goal from Eddie Gaetjens proved England's undoing. Walter Winterbottom's team had missed a hatful of chances, but there was no excuse for such an embarrassing result.

Ten-goal Thriller

Real Madrid 7
Eintracht Frankfurt 3
18 May 1960, Hampden Park, European Cup Final

In the book of unlikely results, a chapter must surely be reserved for the highest-scoring European Cup Final in history. Ten-goal thrillers are infrequent fare at any level of football, so the fact that this festival of scoring came in a European Cup Final makes it all the more remarkable. The match saw the mighty Real Madrid claim their fifth successive continental crown, but it was Eintracht Frankfurt's commendable, though perhaps foolhardy, attacking approach that made it a memorable encounter and scoreline. Eintracht took the lead after 18 minutes but were soon pegged back by a goal from Alfredo Di Stefano. The Argentinian completed his hat trick in the second half – a feat exceeded by Puskas who scored four times. For the record, the other two Eintracht goals both came from veteran winger Kress. The 127,000-strong crowd at Hampden Park patiently waited behind to applaud Real off the field at the end of the game.

Great Comeback

North Korea 3 Portugal 5
23 July 1966, Goodison Park, World Cup finals

A meeting between North Korea and Portugal is not a match that would normally be expected to throw up a classic encounter. However, in 1966, on Merseyside, these two teams produced one of football's most memorable comebacks. North Korea, who had already caused a stir by beating Italy, took a first-minute lead and cruised 3–0 ahead after 30 minutes against Portugal, who had themselves already beaten holders Brazil. However, as every good cliché-wielding commentator knows, it only takes a minute to score a goal and, with an hour left on the clock, Portugal finally woke up. The great Eusebio took control of the match, scoring twice before half-time to bring the Koreans into range. Two more goals from Eusebio after the break took the Portuguese into the lead, before Augusto completed the scoring.

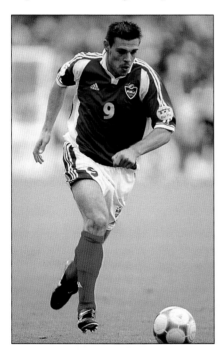

Above: Olé Gunnar Solskjaer scores the dramatic winner in the dying moments of the 1999 European Cup Final.

Below: Savo Milosevic was among Yugoslavia's scorers against Spain.

Late, Late Show

Manchester United 2
Bayern Munich 1
26 May 1999, Camp Nou, European Cup Final

For 90 minutes, the 1999 European Cup Final was in no sense remarkable. Bayern Munich, the slight underdogs, had taken the lead in the ninth minute through Mario Basler and, although both teams had created chances, neither side had added to the scoreline as the match entered stoppage time. Teddy Sheringham was the first to strike for United, turning home a Ryan Giggs cross. Fellow substitute Olé Gunnar Solskjaer then struck the winner deep into added time, after a corner from David Beckham. The Germans were distraught, but for Alex Ferguson's team the frustrations of a stuttering performance were forgotten after a breathtaking three minutes, in which they secured the greatest prize in European club football.

Thriller with a Late Twist

Spain 4 Yugoslavia 3
21 June 2000, Jan Breydel Stadium, Bruges, European Championships

It was the last game of the group stage. Spain had to win and Yugoslavia had only to draw to progress. By half-time Yugoslavia were 2–1 up. Munitis equalized in the second half, but a ten-man Yugoslavia delighted their fans by scoring with 15 minutes to go. On the stroke of normal time, Mendieta equalized with a penalty. Deep into injury time, with Spain pouring forward and Yugoslavia defending desperately, Alfonso sent a half-volley crashing into the Yugoslav net. The whistle went and the final score was 4–3 to Spain, who qualified. The dejected Yugoslav crowd filed out of the stadium, but then came the news that Norway had drawn with Slovenia: Yugoslavia would go through. The party continued late into the night.

World Cup Results

1930 (Uruguay)

The tournament was divided into four groups, with the winners of each group proceeding to the semi-finals.

Semi-finals
Argentina 6 v United States 1
Uruguay 6 v Yugoslavia 1
Final
Uruguay 4 v Argentina 2. Montevideo, 90,000.
Uruguay: Ballesteros, Nasazzi, Mascheroni, Andrade, Fernandez, Gestido, Dorado (1), Scarone, Castro (1), Cea (1), Iriarte (1)
Argentina: Botazzo, Torre, Paternoster, J Evaristo, Monti, Suarez, Peucelle (1), Varallo, Stabile (1), Ferreira, M Evaristo

1934 (Italy)

The format was changed this year to straight knockout between 16 teams.

Semi-finals
Italy 1 v Austria 0
Czechoslovakia 3 v Germany 1

Final
Italy 2 v Czechoslovakia 1; after extra time. Rome, 55,000.
Italy: Combi, Monzeglio, Allemandi, Ferraris, Monti, Bertolini, Guaita, Meazza, Schiavio (1), Ferrari, Orsi (1)
Czechoslovakia: Planicka, Zenisek, Ctyrocky, Kostalek, Cambal, Krcil, Junek, Svoboda, Sobotka, Nejedly, Puc (1)

1938 (France)

Fifteen countries competed for this year's knockout, Sweden receiving a bye in the first round.

Semi-finals
Italy 2 v Brazil 1
Hungary 5 v Sweden 1

Final
Italy 4 v Hungary 2. Paris, 45,000.
Italy: Olivieri, Fona, Rava, Serantoni, Andreolo, Locatelli, Biavati, Meazza, Piola (2), Ferrari, Colaussi (2)
Hungary: Szabo, Polgar, Biro, Szalay, Szucs, Lazar, Sas, Vincze, Sarosi (1), Szengeller, Titkos (1)

1950 (Brazil)

For this year's competition, a league system replaced the knockout format. The authorities had neglected to schedule a final, but fortunately the last game in the league group, Uruguay v Brazil, was the deciding match.

Final pool

	P	W	D	L	F	A	Pts
Uruguay	3	2	1	0	7	5	5
Brazil	3	2	0	1	14	4	4
Sweden	3	1	0	2	6	11	2
Spain	3	0	1	2	4	11	1

Final
Uruguay 2 v Brazil 1. Rio de Janeiro, 199,854.
Uruguay: Maspoli, Gonzalez, Tejera, Gambetta, Varela, Andrade, Ghiggia (1), Perez, Miguez, Schiaffino (1), Moran
Brazil: Barbosa, Augusto, Juvenal, Bauer, Danilo, Bigode, Friaca (1), Zizinho, Ademir, Jair, Chico

1954 (Switzerland)

A knockout system was re-introduced after the group matches.

Semi-finals
Hungary 4 v Uruguay 2
West Germany 6 v Austria 1

Final
West Germany 3 v Hungary 2; after extra time. Berne, 60,000.
West Germany: Turek, Posipal, Kohlmeyer, Eckel, Liebrich, Mai, Rahn (2), Morlock (1), O Walter, F Walter, Schaefer
Hungary: Grosics, Buzansky, Lantos, Bozsik, Zakarias, Lorant, Czibor (1), Kocsis, Hidegkuti, Puskas (1), Toth

1958 (Sweden)

Semi-finals
Brazil 5 v France 2
Sweden 3 v West Germany 1

Final
Brazil 5 v Sweden 2. Stockholm, 47,937.
Brazil: Gilmar, D Santos, N Santos, Zito, Bellini, Orlando, Garrincha, Didi, Vava (2), Pelé (2), Zagallo (1)
Sweden: Svensson, Bergmark, Axbom, Borjesson, Gustavsson, Parling, Hamrin, Gren, Simonsson (1), Liedholm (1), Skoglund

1962 (Chile)

Semi-finals
Brazil 4 v Chile 2
Czechoslovakia 3 v Yugoslavia 1

Final
Brazil 3 v Czechoslovakia 1. Santiago, 68,679.
Brazil: Gilmar, D Santos, N Santos, Zito (1), Mauro, Zozimo, Garrincha, Didi, Vava (1), Amarildo (1), Zagallo
Czechoslovakia: Scroiff, Tichy, Novak, Pluskal, Popluhar, Masopust (1), Pospichal, Scherer, Kvasnak, Kadraba, Jelinek

1966 (England)

Semi-finals
England 2 v Portugal 1
West Germany 2 v USSR 1

Final
England 4 v West Germany 2; after extra time. London, 93,802.
England: Banks, Cohen, Wilson, Stiles, J Charlton, Moore, Ball, Hunt, Hurst (3), R Charlton, Peters (1)
West Germany: Tilkowski, Hottges, Schulz, Weber (1), Schnellinger, Haller (1), Beckenbauer, Overath, Seeler, Held, Emmerich

1970 (Mexico)

Semi-finals
Italy 4 v West Germany 3; after extra time
Brazil 3 v Uruguay 1

Final
Brazil 4 v Italy 1. Mexico City, 107,000.
Brazil: Felix, Carlos Alberto (1), Brito, Piazza, Everaldo, Clodoaldo, Gerson (1), Jairzinho (1), Tostao, Pelé (1), Rivelino
Italy: Albertosi, Burgnich, Cera, Rosato, Facchetti, Bertini (Juliano), Mazzola, De Sisti, Domenghini, Boninsegna (1) (Rivera), Riva

1974 (West Germany)

The winners and second-placed teams in the first four groups moved to a further two groups of four, with the two winners playing each other in the final.

Group A

	P	W	D	L	F	A	Pts
Holland	3	3	0	0	8	0	6
Brazil	3	2	0	1	3	3	4
E Germany	3	0	1	2	1	4	1
Argentina	3	0	1	2	2	7	1

Group B

	P	W	D	L	F	A	Pt
W Germany	3	3	0	0	7	2	6
Poland	3	2	0	1	3	2	4
Sweden	3	1	0	2	4	6	2
Yugoslavia	3	0	0	3	2	6	0

Final

West Germany 2 v Holland 1. Munich, 77,833.
West Germany: Maier, Vogts, Schwarzenbeck, Beckenbauer, Breitner (1 pen), Bonhof, Hoeness, Grabowski, Müller (1), Overath, Holzenbein
Holland: Jongbloed, Suurbier, Rijsbergen (De Jong), Haan, Krol, Jansen, Van Hanegem, Neeskens (1 pen), Rep, Cruyff, Rensenbrink (Van der Kerkhof)

1978 (Argentina)

Group A

	P	W	D	L	F	A	Pts
Holland	3	2	1	0	9	4	5
Italy	3	1	1	1	2	2	3
W Germany	3	0	2	1	4	5	2
Austria	3	1	0	2	4	8	2

Group B

	P	W	D	L	F	A	Pts
Argentina	3	2	1	0	8	0	5
Brazil	3	2	1	0	6	1	5
Poland	3	1	0	2	2	5	2
Peru	3	0	0	3	0	10	0

Final

Argentina 3 v Holland 1; after extra time. Buenos Aires, 77,000.
Argentina: Fillol, Olguin, Galvan, Passarella, Tarantini, Ardiles (Larrosa), Gallego, Ortiz (Houseman), Bertoni (1), Luque, Kempes (2)
Holland: Jongbloed, Jansen (Suurbier), Krol, Brandts, Poortvliet, Haan, Neeskens, W Van der Kerkhov, Rep (Nanninga 1), R Van der Kerkhov, Rensenbrink

1982 (Spain)

The second round was expanded into four groups of three, with the winners proceeding to the semi-finals.

Semi-finals

Italy 2 v Poland 0
West Germany 3 v France 3;
West Germany won 5–4 on penalties

Final

Italy 3 West Germany 1. Madrid, 90,000.
Italy: Zoff, Cabrini, Scirea, Gentile, Collovati, Oriali, Bergomi, Tardelli (1), Conti, Rossi (1), Graziani (Altobelli 1)
West Germany: Schumacher, Kaltz, Stielike, K Forster, B Forster, Breitner (1), Breigel, Dremmler (Hrubesch), Rummenigge (Müller), Littbarski, Fischer

1986 (Mexico)

For this tournament, the league system was dropped for the second round and replaced by knock-outs.

Semi-finals

West Germany 2 v France 0
Argentina 2 v Belgium 0

Final

Argentina 3 v West Germany 2. Mexico City, attendance 115,000.
Argentina: Pumpido, Cuciuffo, Brown (1), Ruggeri, Olarticoechea, Batista, Giusti, Enrique, Burruchaga (1) (Trobbiani), Maradona, Valdano (1)
West Germany: Schumacher, Jakobs, K Forster, Briegel, Brehme, Eder, Berthold, Matthäus, Magath (Hoeness), Rummenigge (1), Allofs (Voller (1))

1990 (Italy)

Semi-finals

Argentina 1 v Italy 1; Argentina won 4–3 on penalties
West Germany 1 v England 1;
West Germany won 4–3 on penalties

Final

West Germany 1 v Argentina 0. Rome, 73,603.
West Germany: Illgner, Berthold (Reuter), Kohler, Augenthaler, Buchwald, Brehme (1), Hassler, Matthäus, Littbarski, Voller, Klinsmann
Argentina: Goycochea, Ruggeri (Monzon), Simon, Serrizuela, Sensini, Basualdo, Burruchaga (Calderon), Troglio, Lorenzo, Maradona, Dezotti

1994 (USA)

Semi-finals

Italy 2 v Bulgaria 1
Brazil 1 v Sweden 0

Final

Brazil 0 v Italy 0; Brazil won 3–2 on penalties. Pasadena, 94,000.
Brazil: Taffarel, Jorghino (Cafu), Aldair, Marcio Santos, Branco, Mazinho, Mauro Silva, Dunga, Zinho (Viola), Romario, Bebeto
Italy: Pagliuca, Mussi (Apolloni), Baresi, Maldini, Benarrivo, Berti, Albertini, D Baggio (Evani), Donadoni, R Baggio, Massaro
Penalty shoot-out: Baresi misses, 0–0; Marcio Santos misses, 0–0; Albertini scores, 0–1; Romario scores, 1–1; Evani scores, 1–2; Branco scores, 2–2; Massaro misses, 2–2; Dunga scores, 3–2; R Baggio misses 3–2.

1998 (France)

Semi-finals

Brazil 1 v Holland 1; Brazil won 4–2 on penalties
France 2 v Croatia 1

Final

France 3 v Brazil 0. St Denis, Paris, 75,000.
France: Barthez, Thuram, Leboeuf, Desailly, Lizarazu, Karembeu (Boghossian), Deschamps, Zidane (2), Petit (1), Djorkaeff (Vieira), Guivarc'h (Dugarry)
Brazil: Taffarel, Cafu, Aldair, Baiano, Roberto Carlos, Leonardo (Denilson), Cesar Sampaio (Edmundo), Dunga, Rivaldo, Ronaldo, Bebeto

2002 (Japan and South Korea)

Semi-finals

Brazil 1 v Turkey 0
Germany 1 v South Korea 0

Final

Brazil 2 v Germany 0. Yokohama, 69,029.
Brazil: Marcos, Lucio, Roque Junior, Edmilson, Cafu, Kleberson, Gilberto Silva, Roberto Carlos, Rivaldo, Ronaldinho (Juninho), Ronaldo (2) (Denilson)
Germany: Kahn, Linke, Ramelow, Metzelder, Frings, Schneider, Hamann, Jeremies (Asamoah), Bode (Ziege), Neuville, Klose (Bierhoff)

International Results

EUROPEAN CHAMPIONSHIP

1960
USSR 2 v Yugoslavia 1. Paris, 18,000.
USSR: Yashin, Tchekeli, Kroutilov, Voinov, Maslenkin, Netto, Metreveli (1), Ivanov, Ponedelnik (1), Bubukin, Meshki
Yugoslavia: Vidinic, Durkovic, Zanetic, Jusufi, Miladinovic, Perusic, Sekularac, Jerkovic, Matus, Galic (1), Kostic

1964
Spain 2 v USSR 1. Madrid, 120,000.
Spain: Iribar, Olivella, Rivilla, Calleja, Fuste, Zoco, Pereda (1), Marcelino (1), Amancio, Suarez, Lapetra
USSR: Yashin, Chustikov, Mudrik, Voronin, Shesterniev, Chislenko, Anitchkin, Ivanov, Kornalev, Ponedelnik, Khusainov (1)

1968
Yugoslavia 1 v Italy 1; after extra time. Replay Italy 2 v Yugoslavia 0. Rome, 75,000.
Italy: Zoff, Burgnich, Rosato, Guarneri, Facchetti, Salvadore, Domenghini, Anastasi (1), Mazzola, De Sisti, Riva (1)
Yugoslavia: Pantelic, Fazlagic, Damjanovic, Pavlovic, Holcer, Hosic, Paunovic, Acimovic, Trivic, Musemic, Dzajic

1972
West Germany 3 v USSR 0. Brussels, 43,000.
West Germany: Maier, Hottges, Schwarzenbeck, Beckenbauer, Breitner, Wimmer (1), Netzer, Hoeness, Heynckes, Müller (2), Kremers
USSR: Rudakov, Dzodzuashvili, Khurtislava, Istomin, Troshkin, Kaplichny, Kolotov, Konkov (Dolmatov), Baidachini, Banishevsky (Kozinkievits), Oninshenko

1976
Czechoslovakia 2 v West Germany 2; Czechoslovakia won 5–3 on penalties. Belgrade, 45,000.
Czechoslovakia: Viktor, Dobias (1) (Vesely), Capkovic, Ondrus, Pivarnik, Gogh, Moder, Panenka, Svehlik (1) (Jurkemik), Masny, Nehoda
West Germany: Maier, Beckenbauer, Schwarzenbeck, Dietz, Voigts, Bonhof, Wimmer (Flohe), Müller (1), Beer (Bongartz), Hoeness, Holzenbein (1)

1980
West Germany 2 v Belgium 1. Rome, 48,000.
West Germany: Schumacher, Kalz, Forster, Stielike, Dietz, Briegel (Cullman), Schuster, Müller, Rummenigge, Hrubesch (2), Allofs
Belgium: Pfaff, Gerets, Millecamps Meeuws, Renquin, Van Moer, Cools, Vandereycken (1), Van der Elst, Mommens, Ceulemans

1984
France 2 v Spain 0. Paris, 48,000.
France: Bats, Battiston (Amoros), Le Roux, Bossis, Domergue, Fernandez, Tigana, Giresse, Platini (1), Lacombe (Genghini), Bellone (1)
Spain: Arconada, Urquiaga, Salva (Roberto), Gallego, Julio Alberto (Sarabia), Senor, Victor, Camacho, Francisco, Santillana, Carrasco

1988
Holland 2 v Soviet Union 0. Munich, 72,000.
Holland: Van Breukelen, Van Aerle, Rijkaard, R Koeman, Van Tiggelen, Vanenburg, Wouters, Muhren, E Koeman, Gullit (1), Van Basten (1)
Soviet Union:

1992
Denmark 2 v Germany 0. Gothenburg, 38,000.
Denmark: Schmeichel, Piechnik, Olsen, Nielsen, Sivebaek (Christiansen), Vilfort (1), Jensen (1), Larsen, Christofte, Povlsen, Laudrup
Germany: Illgner, Reuter, Helmer, Buchwald, Kohler, Hassler, Effenberg (Thom), Sammer (Doll), Brehme, Klinsmann, Riedle

1996
Germany 2 v Czech Republic 1. London, 74,000.
Germany: Kopke, Helmer, Babbel, Struntz, Sammer, Scholl (Bierhof 2), Eilts (Bode), Hassler, Ziege, Kuntz, Klinsmann
Czech Republic: Kouba, Rada, Kadlec, Suchoparek, Bejbl, Hornak, Nedved, Nemec, Berger (1pen), Poborsky (Smicer), Kuka

2000
France 2 v Italy 1; "golden goal" in extra time. Rotterdam, 51,000.
France: Barthez, Thuram, Blanc, Desailly, Lizarazu (Pires), Dugarry (Wiltord 1), Vieira, Deschamps, Zidane, Djorkaeff (Trezeguet 1), Henry
Italy: Toldo, Maldini, Juliano, Nesta, Cannavaro, Flore (Del Piero), Albertini, Di Bagio (Ambrosini), Pessotto, Totti, Delvecchio (1)

EUROPEAN CUP
(from 1992–93 also called the Champions League)

1956 Real Madrid 4 (Di Stefano, Rial 2, Marquitos) v Reims 3 (Le Blond, Templin, Hidalgo). Paris, 38,000.
1957 Real Madrid 2 (Di Stefano, Gento) v Fiorentina 0. Madrid, 124,000.
1958 Real Madrid 3 (Di Stefano, Rial, Gento) v AC Milan 2 (Schiffiano, Grillo); after extra time. Brussels, 70,000.
1959 Real Madrid 2 (Matteos, Di Stefano) v Reims 0. Stuttgart, 72,000.
1960 Real Madrid 7 (Di Stefano 3, Puskas 4) v Eintracht Frankfurt 3 (Kress, Stein 2). Glasgow, 127,000.
1961 Benfica 3 (Aguas, Ramallets og, Coluna) v Barcelona 2 (Kocsis, Czibor). Berne, 27,000.
1962 Benfica 5 (Aguas, Cavem, Coluna, Eusebio 3) v Real Madrid 3 (Puskas 3). Amsterdam, 61,000.
1963 AC Milan 2 (Altafini 2) v Benfica 1 (Eusebio). London, 45,000.
1964 Internazionale 3 (Mazzola 2, Milani) v Real Madrid 1 (Feola). Vienna, 71,000.
1965 Internazionale 1 (Jair) v Benfica 0. Milan, 89,000.
1966 Real Madrid 2 (Amancio, Serena) v Partizan Belgrade 1 (Vasovic). Brussels, 46,000.
1967 Celtic 2 (Gemmell, Chalmers) v Internazionale 1 (Mazzola). Lisbon, 56,000.
1968 Manchester United 4 (Charlton 2, Best, Kidd) v Benfica 1 (Graca); after extra time. London, 100,000.
1969 AC Milan 4 (Prati 3, Sormani) v Ajax 1 (Vasovic). Madrid, 32,000.
1970 Feyenoord 2 (Israel, Kindvaal) v Celtic 1 (Gemmell). Milan, 53,000.
1971 Ajax 2 (Van Dijk, Haan) v Panathinaikos 0. London, 83,000.
1972 Ajax 2 (Cruyff 2) v Internazionale 0. Rotterdam, 61,000.
1973 Ajax 1 (Rep) v Juventus 0. Belgrade, 90,000.
1974 Bayern Munich 1 (Schwarzenbeck) v Atlético Madrid 1 (Aragones). Brussels, 49,000.
1974 (replay) Bayern Munich 4 (Hoeness 2, Müller 2) v Atlético Madrid 0. Brussels, 23,000.
1975 Bayern Munich 2 (Roth, Müller) v Leeds United 0. Paris, 50,000.
1976 Bayern Munich 1 (Roth) v Saint Etienne 0. Glasgow, 55,000.
1977 Liverpool 3 (McDermott, Smith, Neal) v Borussia Mönchengladbach 1 (Simonsen). Rome, 52,000.
1978 Liverpool 1 (Dalglish) v Bruges 0. London, 92,000.
1979 Nottingham Forest 1 (Francis) v Malmo 0. Munich, 57,000.
1980 Nottingham Forest 1 (Robertson) v Hamburg 0. Madrid, 50,000.
1981 Liverpool 1 (A Kennedy) v Real Madrid 0. Paris, 48,000.
1982 Aston Villa 1 (Withe) v Bayern Munich 0. Rotterdam, 46,000.
1983 Hamburg 1 (Magath) v Juventus 0. Athens, 75,000.
1984 Liverpool 1 (Neal) v Roma 1 (Pruzzo); Liverpool won 4–2 on penalties. Rome, 70,000.
1985 Juventus 1 (Platini) v Liverpool 0. Brussels, 50,000.
1986 Steaua Bucharest 0 v Barcelona 0; Staeua won 2–0 on penalties. Seville, 50,000.